CONTENTS

BRAIN FITNESS

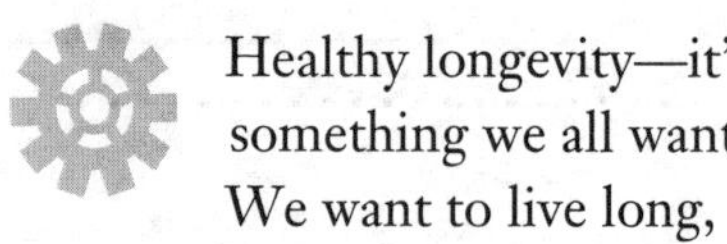

Healthy longevity—it's something we all want. We want to live long, full lives and maintain our independence for as long as possible. To do this, we must keep our bodies and minds in good working order. Sounds straightforward enough. And over the last 20 or 25 years, the popular media have eagerly stepped up to report the latest research and recommendations on how to keep our bodies in healthy shape. But only very recently has there been much mainstream mention of how to maintain a well-functioning and healthy mind. That's why this guide is so important and so valuable. This book is designed to start filling that coverage gap and provide you with brain-challenging puzzles and mental exercises that can help you train your brain and keep it "fit" for years to come.

Most people know that one of the keys to living a long, healthy life is a physically fit body. And it's pretty much common knowledge that to achieve and maintain physical fitness, we have to stay active and watch what and how much we eat. Walking, swimming, and other exercises, we've been told, are excellent ways to keep our bodies in shape as time passes.

We've also been clued in to the importance of emotional fitness for a healthy body and longevity. Research has indicated that we need to connect with family and friends, have good support networks, and make time for fun and laughter—not only to minimize stress and depression but to prevent the very real negative effects that these states can have on our bodies (including heart, blood-vessel, and immune-system damage). Volunteering, participating in group activities, and keeping in touch with friends and family are a few of the habits we've been encouraged to adopt to protect and enhance our emotional fitness and resilience.

Yet despite all the news and advice we've been given over the years about keeping ourselves fit for life, one extremely important element of healthy longevity has only very recently begun to get the attention it deserves. That essential component is cognitive fitness—keeping our brains stimulated, active, and functioning well, now and for years to come. It seems almost unbelievable that the search for ways to enhance and preserve such a vital aspect of our "selves" should have been so badly neglected for so long. After all, the brain is not only the "control center" of the body, it is the storehouse of our memories, the seat of all learning, and the organ that actually allows us to contemplate healthy longevity in the first place. Fortunately, the spotlight has finally begun to fall "on our heads."

So, how can you stay cognitively fit? The first thing to do is let go of any fear that "you can't teach an old dog new tricks." One of the most exciting discoveries made through the use of new imaging technology is that, contrary to a belief long-held among scientists, the adult human brain can and does generate new neurons, or brain cells. What's more, research has shown that people who are reminded of negative stereotypes about aging—that aging inevitably brings memory loss, confusion, and frailty, for example—actually do worse on subsequent memory tests. In other words, believing negative things about aging can actually become a self-fulfilling prophecy. On the other hand, studies have shown that people with positive opinions and expectations of their "mature years" tend to be healthier and more cognitively fit as they age. Therefore, if you want to stay mentally fit throughout life, you first need to believe that you can take measures to make that happen. Picking up this book is certainly a step in the right direction.

Another important step in maintaining cognitive fitness is to be aware that your brain—and therefore your cognitive ability—benefits from many of the same lifestyle measures that are essential for physical fitness. That's right. A growing pool of research indicates that regular physical activity and a varied, balanced, nutritious diet are important for healthy brain function. Likewise, a burst of new research suggests that healthy eating habits—getting plenty of vegetables, fruits, cereals, and legumes; eating only moderate to low amounts of dairy, fish, and poultry; avoiding or severely limiting red meat and eggs; and using olive oil as the dominant source of fat—may help fend off Alzheimer's disease.

But if you're really serious about maintaining your cognitive fitness, you need to do more than keep a positive attitude and healthy fitness habits. You have to get your head in the game (pun intended). "Use it or lose it!" needs to become your motto from now on. And the brain games in this book are a great place to start.

You need to keep in mind that the brain loves to learn and to experience new things—it is stimulated by novelty, and it thrives on challenge. If something is routine or too easy, our brains are not challenged and we are essentially operating on autopilot, which does not require a lot of thought and does little to maintain cognitive fitness. Therefore, we need to find ways to exercise our brains, keeping them sharp, strong, and fit. Learning and trying new things stimulates the brain. Whether you attempt to learn a new language, a new knitting technique, or how to square dance, you are giving your brain a workout. The more you have to think and remember, the more you are exercising your brain. If something is easy, your brain is not working hard enough. On the other hand, if something is too difficult, you can become frustrated and give up, and then the brain gets little or no workout.

We all know that puzzles are fun to solve, but are they good for our brains? Most experts agree that they are. Many gerontologists and physicians recommend working puzzles as one way of retaining mental flexibility. Puzzles require focused attention and concentration, help increase mental flexibility, and require the use of problem-solving skills, all of which are important cognitive functions. We can think of puzzles as mini workouts for our brains, and if this is the case, we should try to maximize the benefit that we get from these mental workouts. How do we do this? Let's look at a few tips that will help you use puzzles to get the best brain workout possible.

First things first—spend a minute or two selecting the type of puzzle and the level of difficulty. There are many different types of puzzles, and most people just choose a puzzle that they like to do and one that they can probably finish rather easily. This is fine if you are using the puzzles for entertainment. However, if you want to maximize your brain workout, you need to use a little more care in the selection process. The brain loves novelty, so try not to work the same kind of puzzle day after day. Different types of puzzles stimulate different parts of the brain, and you want to work as many of these parts as possible. To help in your selection, we've labeled each puzzle with the cognitive function(s) it exercises. Consider doing a few different types of puzzles each day. If you only work crossword puzzles, for example, you may get very good at solving this type of puzzle, but you are limiting the scope of your workout. Choose puzzles that make you think. Like physical fitness, cognitive fitness can be the result of consistently challenging workouts.

Don't forget that puzzles are portable. They can travel with you to the park, the beach, or the dentist's office. Why not turn your downtime into brain-boosting time? It can also be enjoyable working puzzles with other people. This is a great way to keep emotionally fit. So, the next time you want to give yourself a physical, emotional, and cognitive workout, grab that puzzle book, walk over to a friend's house, and get to work. Oh, and don't forget—have fun!

GETTING STARTED

LEVEL 1

Crosswise

ATTENTION LANGUAGE VISUAL SEARCH

Every word listed is contained within the group of letters below. The words can be found in a straight line horizontally, vertically, or diagonally. The words can be read either backward or forward.

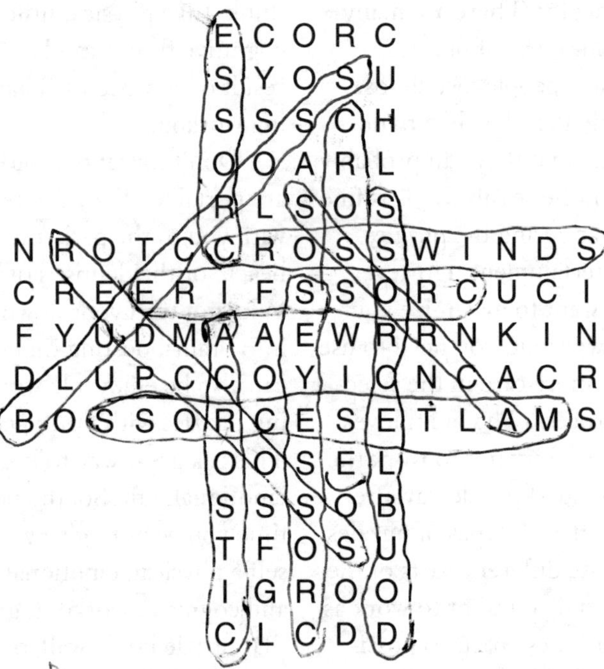

ACROSS	CROSS-EYES	DOUBLE CROSS
ACROSTIC	CROSS FIRE	MALTESE CROSS
BLUE CROSS	CROSSWINDS	RED CROSS
CROSSE	CROSSWISE	

Answers on page 85.

It Figures

COMPUTATION LOGIC

Fill each square in the grid with a digit from 1 through 9. When the numbers in each row are added, you should arrive at the total in the right-hand column. When the numbers in each column are added, you should arrive at the total on the bottom line. The numbers in each diagonal must add up to the totals in the upper and lower right corners.

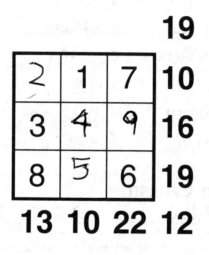

			19
	1	7	10
3			16
8		6	19
13	10	22	12

Dry Your Eyes

LANGUAGE

Can you "read" the phrase below?

DON'T CRY

SPILLED MILK

Answers on page 85.

In a Stew

LANGUAGE

It's dinnertime! Can you unscramble the ingredients for the stew?

RACTOR	______
RUPINT	______
ATASP	______
TOOTAP	______
SEINASONG	______
KELE	______
CENICHK	______
CRYLEE	______

Thinking Outside the Bubbles

LANGUAGE

Rearrange the 4 groups of letters to form one word.

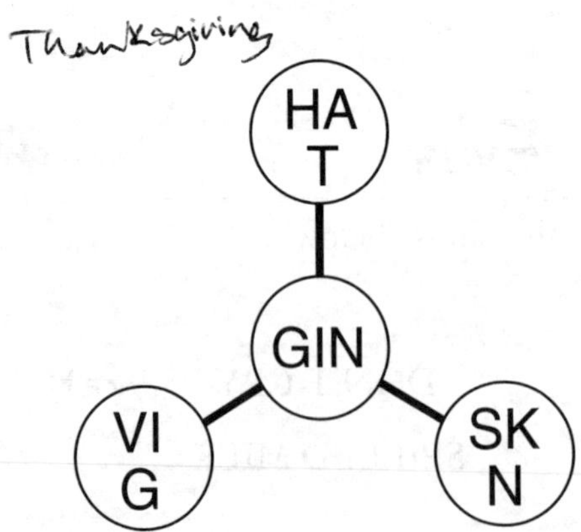

Answers on page 85.

Number Climber

COMPUTATION LOGIC

Help the mountaineer reach the summit by filling the boulder circles with numbers. Each boulder is the sum (the total when added) of the 2 numbers in the boulders that support it. For example: 2+3=5. If a total is 10 or more, only write in the second digit. For example: 7+6=13; write in 3.

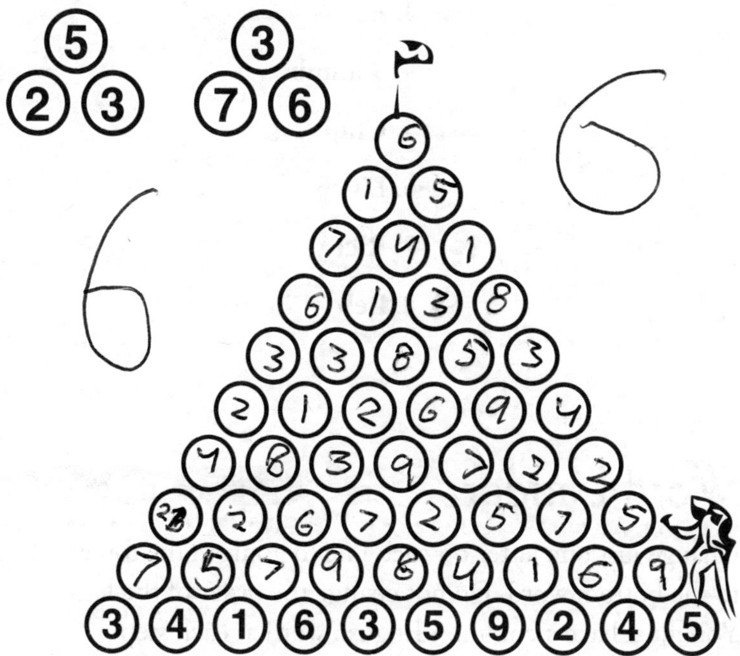

It's Thrilling!

LANGUAGE

Can you "read" the phrase below?

SUDDEN DEATH

TIME

Answers on page 85.

Colorful Phrases

LANGUAGE

Something about each word should suggest a common phrase to you. What are the phrases?

1. **Carpet**
2. **Blossom**
3. **Pages**
4. **Thumb**
5. **Chip**
6. **Finch**
7. **Rice**
8. **Belt**

Word Ladder

LOGIC PLANNING

Change just one letter on each line to go from the top word to the bottom word. Do not change the order of the letters. You must have a common English word at each step.

HATE

Have

cave

cove

LOVE

Answers on page 85.

Donut Maze

PLANNING SPATIAL REASONING

Nothing eases the Monday-morning blues like a donut. If you can find your way through this maze, you'll be on your way to a great week!

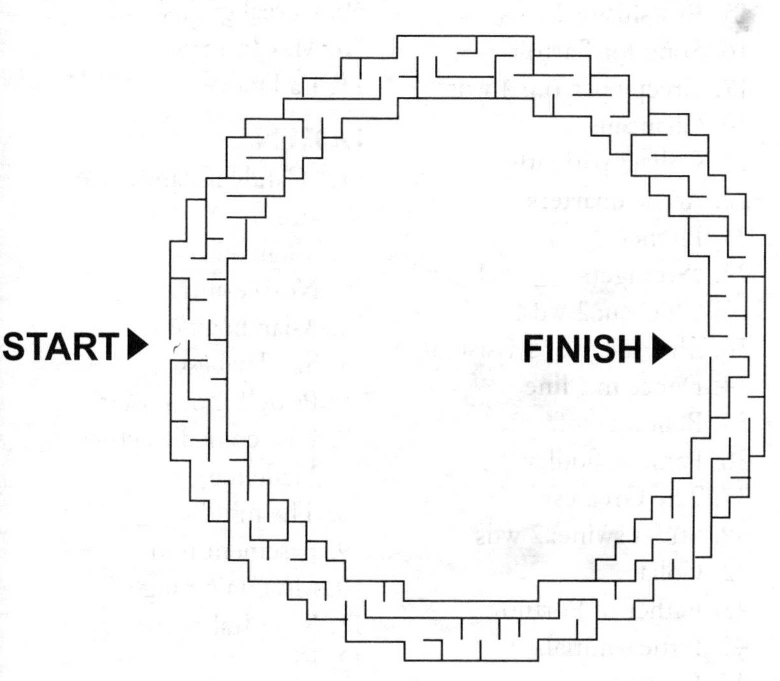

Answer on page 85.

Zoo Story

GENERAL KNOWLEDGE LANGUAGE

ACROSS

1. Former Cleveland pitcher Charles
5. Phony
9. Belch
13. Yearly record
15. Britishism: 2 wds.
16. Song for Bartoli
17. Creepy person: 4 wds.
20. Chapeau
21. Collect patiently
22. Arctic quarters
23. Pitcher
24. "Strangers _____ Train"
25. Chicken: 2 wds.
30. Mad scientist's assistant
34. Dance in a line
35. Believer: suf.
36. Famous fiddler
37. The Greatest
38. Street swine: 2 wds.
42. Collar
43. Father of Portnoy
45. Fifties' initials
46. Lenya
48. Lady of the haus: Ger.
49. Overnight stars, in a way: 2 wds.
52. Appliance store items: abbr.
54. Regatta sights
55. Tend to the turkey
58. Domineering
60. Auto club initials
63. Relatives of the paparazzi: 2 wds.
66. The Shah's former country
67. Theater award
68. Sideshow attraction
69. Cereal grains
70. Max Jr. or Sr.
71. La Douce

DOWN

1. "Candy is dandy..." author
2. Magnani
3. No-see-um
4. Asian bovine
5. Sunday best
6. Powell–Loy costar
7. Late comedic actor Madeline
8. The mind's _____
9. Basement find
10. Mountain range
11. Rice: Ital.
12. El _____
14. Stockings, e.g.
18. "_____ Three Lives"
19. Cheever's "The Sorrows of _____"
23. Work unit
24. Von Bismarck
25. What you place around your neck
26. Tint
27. Loos or Ekberg

28. Fall drink
29. Ember
31. Ladies' escorts, for short
32. Speak
33. Kimonos
39. Tout's figures
40. Nabokov novel
41. "That's the story of, that's the _____ love"
44. Jim and Tim
47. Conjunctions
50. Blessed by the rabbi
51. Corned beef seconds
53. Relax; do nothing: sl.
55. TV's Chachi
56. Air
57. Sports fig.
58. Rum cake
59. Ron Howard role
60. Biblical name
61. First fellow
62. _____ silly question . . .
64. Reiner
65. Site of the William Tell legend

Answers on page 85.

Rhyme Time: See Me

GENERAL KNOWLEDGE

LANGUAGE

Answer each clue below with a pair of rhyming words. The numbers that follow each clue indicate how many letters are in each word. We've done the first one for you.

1. Order from the boss (3, 2): **see me**
2. Police chief (3, 3): ________________
3. Poor hitter's aide (3, 3): ________________
4. Dinner call (4, 3): ________________
5. Previous year's performers (4, 4) ________________
6. Young horse's pal (4, 5): ________________
7. Despots on the red planet (4, 5): ________________
8. Another left sandal (5, 5): ________________
9. Candy with fresh-brewed flavor (6, 6): ________________
10. Parts of news shows (6, 7): ________________

Times Square

COMPUTATION

LOGIC

Fill each square in the grid with a digit from 1 through 9. When the numbers in each row are multiplied, you should arrive at the total in the right-hand column. When the numbers in each column are multiplied, you should arrive at the total on the bottom line. Important: The number 1 can only be used once in any row or column; other numbers can be repeated.

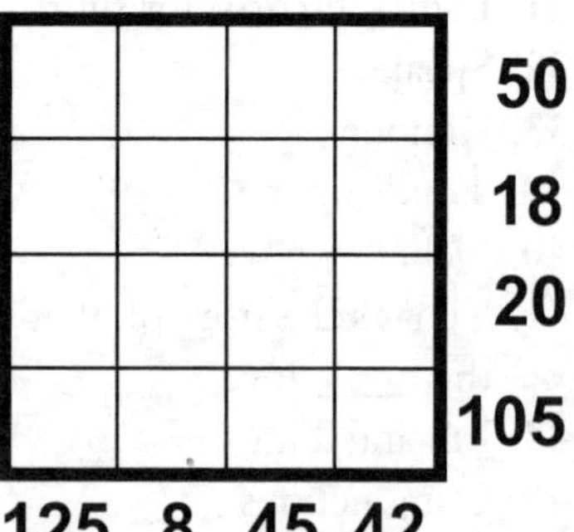

Hint: Some of the grid squares contain 5's and 7's. Identify these first.

Answers on page 86.

Counting Candy

CREATIVE THINKING | LOGIC

Twins Andy and Randy shared everything equally. On Halloween, Andy ran from house to house getting candy while Randy stopped to smell the flowers. At the end of the night, they compared the number of pieces of candy in each bag. “We share everything equally,” said Randy. “You have three times as many pieces of candy as I do.” Andy was upset but handed over 20 pieces. “I said we share everything equally,” said the flower-sniffing-and-candy-loving Randy. “You still have twice as many pieces of candy as I do.” In order for the twins to have equal pieces of candy, how many more must Andy give to Randy? How many did each have at the start?

Initially Yours

GENERAL KNOWLEDGE | LANGUAGE

We hope you don’t come up short trying to figure out what these famous abbreviations stand for!

1. BMOC, at a college
2. BOMC, a famous mail-order company
3. COD, in parcel post
4. ESP, in parapsychology
5. HDTV
6. MGS, in weather reports about skiing conditions
7. PT, as in PT boat
8. SRO, in the theatre
9. UFO
10. WD, in the product name WD-40

Answers on page 86.

Really Sum-thing

COMPUTATION LOGIC

Fill each square in the grid with a digit from 1 through 9. When the numbers in each row are added, you should arrive at the total in the right-hand column. When the numbers in each column are added, you should arrive at the total on the bottom line. The numbers in each diagonal must add up to the totals in the upper and lower right corners.

			9
7	9		19
8	1		13
	2		13
20	12	13	14

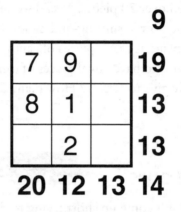

Go for the Gourd

ATTENTION LANGUAGE

Find all occurrences of the word "go" in the following paragraph.

Gomer got the urge to drag out an orange gourd even though it wasn't Halloween. He carved his own face (which shows that his ego was a big one!). Gomer got more gourds and carved a goose with gout, an egg on a wall, and a gang of gorillas going ape. He showed them to his gal Gloria, a former go-go dancer who was now a big old gourd grower from Georgia. She gave Gomer a bag of seeds to grow more gourds and go whole-hog out on his porch carving them.

Answers on page 86.

21 Is a "Sharp" Number

COMPUTATION

Blacken any 2 triangles that share a common side and have numbers that add up to 21. When you are finished, you will discover the meaning of the puzzle title.

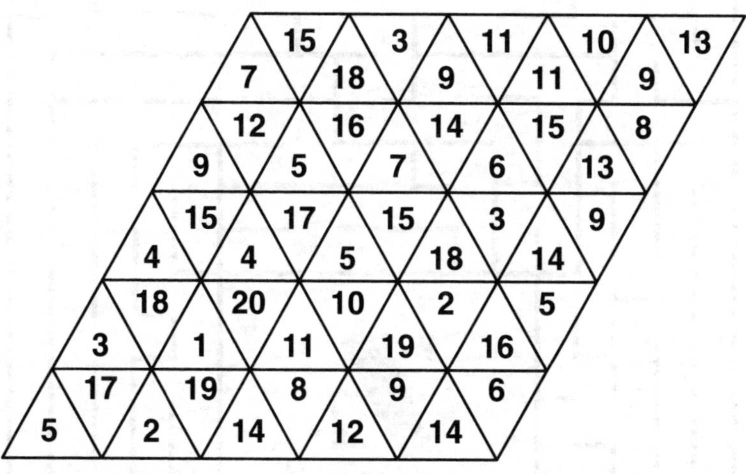

Time Will Tell

LANGUAGE

Can you "read" the phrase below?

WAITC

Answers on page 86.

A-MAZE-ing Race

PLANNING SPATIAL REASONING

Can you get from Alaska to Zanzibar? Actually, we'll settle for A to Z.

Answer on page 86.

True or False

ATTENTION COMPUTATION

Each group of scrambled letters can be rearranged to reveal a number word. Following the mathematical functions indicated, mark each problem true or false. For example, Problem No. 1: 4+5=8 is false.

1. ORFU+VIFE=HIGET
2. REHET+VEENEL=ERONETUF
3. TETOWWYNT−TINNENEE=OWT
4. EFFENIT+NEXTIES=HORINTTEY
5. TINNEY−VETELW=GHYTIGETHIE
6. FYTVORIFE−TROFY=XYROFIST
7. VESNE+NELVEE=INEGETHE
8. HYGITE−TYNEWT=NETYVES
9. TENSYEV+HERITTEN=THETHIGREEY
10. HONIRTTYE−OTEWENYNT=WELTEV

Answers on page 87.

Initially Yours

GENERAL KNOWLEDGE LANGUAGE

We hope you don't come up short trying to figure out what these famous abbreviations stand for!

1. B&O, the railroad
2. CARE, the foreign-aid organization
3. ECG, at a hospital
4. GMT
5. ISBN, to a librarian
6. LED, in electronics
7. NASA
8. RSVP, on an invitation
9. SAM, the military weapon
10. SWAK, on a love letter

Word Ladder

LANGUAGE PLANNING

Change just one letter on each line to go from the top word to the bottom word. Do not change the order of the letters. You must have a common English word at each step.

DOVE

______ profound affection

______ traditional knowledge

______ to tempt

______ to wait secretly

LARK

Answers on page 87.

STRETCH YOUR BRAIN 

Spinning in Circles PLANNING SPATIAL REASONING

Connect the dots by finding your way through this circular maze.

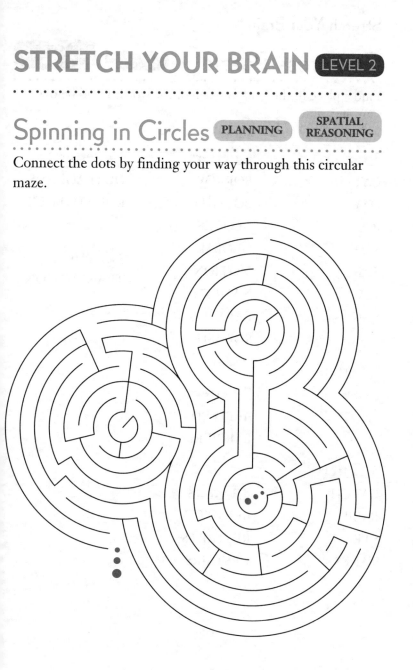

Answer on page 87.

Crisscross Puzzle

LOGIC | SPATIAL REASONING

Find a place in the grid for each of the words listed below.

3 Letters
CAT
DAY
ICE
SAD
TAB
VIA
VAN

4 Letters
NOSE
SHOT

5 Letters
CATCH
RABID
STEAM
TAKES

6 Letters
BORROW
BOUGHT
CLOCKS
GLOBAL
MOTION
NAMING
REPAIR
SQUASH

7 Letters
ARRIVED
BARRIER

8 Letters
BRIGHTLY
RESTARTS
UPSTAIRS

10 Letters
OUTRAGEOUS
ROUNDABOUT

11 Letters
TRANSACTION

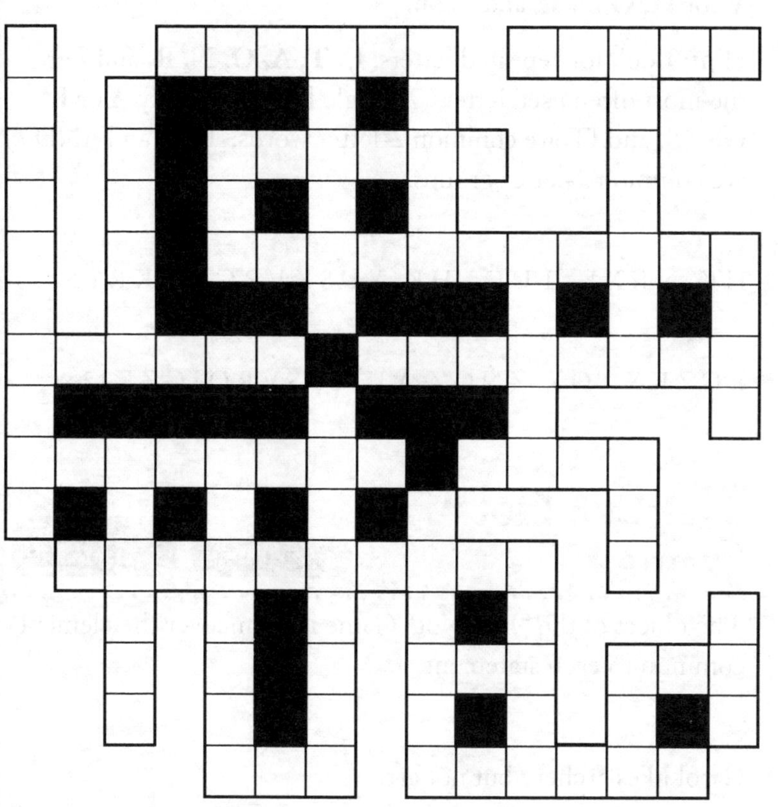

Answers on page 87.

Zen in a Nutshell

LANGUAGE LOGIC

Cryptograms are messages in substitution code. Break the code to read the message. For example, THE SMART CAT might become FVO QWGDF JGF if **F** is substituted for **T, V** for **H, O** for **E,** and so on.

Hint: Look for repeated letters. **E, T, A, O, N, R,** and **I** are the most often used letters. A single letter is usually **A** or **I;** OF, IS, and IT are common 2-letter words; THE and AND are common 3-letter groups.

HK NKXK TUC. HK YUSKVRGIK KRYK

RGZKX. OY ZNGZ YU IUSVROIGZKJ?

The But-Not Game

LANGUAGE VERBAL REASONING

The object of the "But-Not" Game is to uncover the element common to each statement.

Carol likes archery but not arrows.

Carol likes brothers but not sisters.

Carol likes fishers but not fish.

So ... what does Carol like?

Answers on page 87.

Reach the "Sum"mit

COMPUTATION LOGIC

Help the mountaineer reach the summit by filling in the boulder circles with numbers. Each boulder is the sum (the total when added) of the two numbers in the boulders that support it. For example: 2+3=5. If a total is 10 or more, only write in the second digit. For example: 7+6=13; write in 3.

Answers on page 87.

ATTENTION LANGUAGE VISUAL SEARCH

Food for Thought

Every word or phrase listed is contained within the group of letters on the next page. Words can be found in a straight line horizontally, vertically, or diagonally. The words can be read either backward or forward.

As an added challenge try to figure out the theme of this puzzle.

BEAR FRUIT
BIG CHEESE
BIRTHDAY SUIT
CARROT AND STICK
COFFEE BEANS
CRAB NEBULA
ENGLISH POUND
FLASH IN THE PAN
GO FISH
HARD ROW TO HOE
HOT PURSUIT
JOHNNY REB
MARBLE COLUMN
NOT MY CUP OF TEA
OATER
OZONE LAYER
PATTY DUKE
RICE UNIVERSITY
RUMMY
SHORT LIST
SPONGE BATH
WEDDING GOWN
WHERE'S THE BEEF?

```
      E A C H C T T H W O R C
      D O R B S R O I R E A X
      W E P I I T A N U R R R
E S F T H L S P R W B R R N U I O N
I N A L T E U O O T O N M F C M Y C
L O A R A R R G Z T H U E O R T M E
U H O E S S G E A O L D F B I A N Y
D H A U T N H N S O N F A S U G E E
S B I R I F D I C T E E R Y L L H B
B T I D D S O E N E H E L I S T A E
S E D G T R L P B T V E S A A U K A
H E R I C B O E U I H H B B Y U I W
W S C Y R H A W N C P E E E D E O T
R K I A N N E U T O Y G P Y E D R T
H A M F S N E E U O N M T A T F I S
      A O C H N S O H T T T N
      Y I G D O P E A O P O E
      R O F C S J P A K E E N
```

Answers on page 88.

Mirror, Mirror

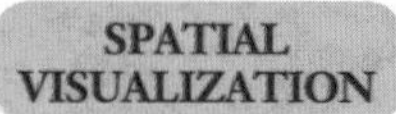

There's no trick here, only a challenge: Draw the mirror image of these familiar objects. You may find it harder than you think!

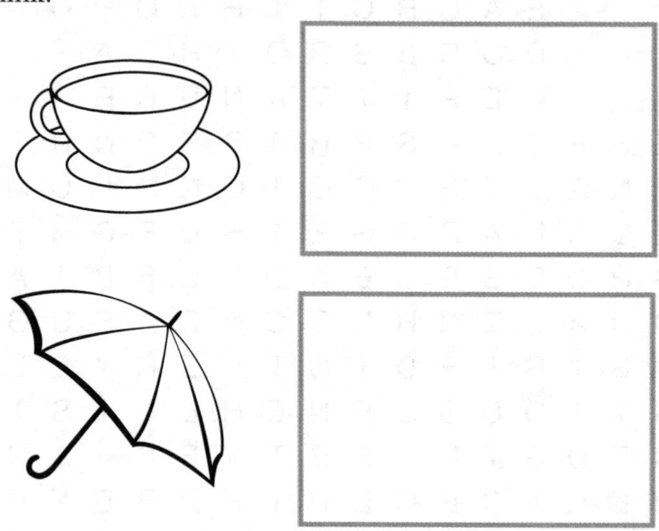

Making Music

LANGUAGE

Can you "read" the phrase below?

L
O
A
D
S
O
N
G
S

Answer on page 88.

The Times Tables Are Turned!

COMPUTATION LOGIC

Fill each square of the grid with a digit from 1 through 9. When the numbers in each row are multipled, you should arrive at the total in the right-hand column. When the numbers in each column are multiplied, you should arrive at the total on the bottom line. The numbers in each diagonal must multiply to the totals in the upper and lower right corners. Important: The number 1 can only be used once in any row or column; other numbers can be repeated.

			75
	3		30
	5	4	80
3			6
24	15	40	20

Picnic Puzzle

COMPUTATION LOGIC

Sally was preparing a picnic lunch for her hungry family. First, she covered the square table with a red-and-white checkerboard tablecloth that had 64 squares. Then she put a pitcher of lemonade in each of 2 diagonal corners. She had a plate of 31 hoagie sandwiches, each one big enough to cover 2 squares of the tablecloth. Sally wanted to put the hoagies on the tablecloth and cover the remaining 62 squares with no hoagies overlapping, none hanging over the edge of the table, and none standing on end. Was she able to figure out a way to do it before her hungry family showed up to eat them?

Answers on page 88.

Stretch Your Brain

Breakfast's Ready

GENERAL KNOWLEDGE | LANGUAGE

ACROSS

1. Pursue
6. Oak nut
11. Possessed
14. Surround: 2 wds.
15. Recipient
16. Lincoln
17. Breakfast item: 2 wds.
19. Me: Fr.
20. Hit in the head
21. Actor Reynolds
22. Sleepy or Doc
24. Emcee
25. Enough
26. Bewitch
30. Collie or poodle, e.g.
31. Confirm
32. Rapture
33. Recede
36. Be
37. Stir
38. Motherless calf
40. Privileges: abbr.
41. Profession
42. Low bubbling sound
43. Sat for the painter
46. Hair
47. Commotion
49. Mardi _____
50. Use
51. _____ Day (Feb. 29)
52. Accountants: abbr.
56. French title of nobility
57. Breakfast item: 2 wds.
60. Initials of a classic rock group
61. Not suitable
62. Friendship
63. _____ Francisco
64. Assessments
65. Take it easy

DOWN

1. Ice cream flavor: abbr.
2. Protagonist
3. "_____ for All Seasons"
4. Piece of plumbing
5. Elizabeth's land: abbr.
6. Adapt
7. Tennis area
8. "Sit _____!"
9. Part of R & R: abbr.
10. Tool for a seamstress
11. Breakfast items: 3 wds.
12. Scrap a space project
13. Make into a god
18. Black wood
23. Tiny
24. Sword handle
25. Use a crowbar
26. Always
27. Succeeding
28. Breakfast item: 2 wds.
29. Towel designation
30. Carton

1	2	3	4	5	■	6	7	8	9	10	■	11	12	13
14					■	15					■	16		
17					18						■	19		
20				■	21				■	22	23			
■	■	■	■	24				■	25					
26	27	28	29				■	30					■	■
31						■	32			■	■	33	34	35
36					■	37			■	38	39			
40			■	■	41			■	42					
■	■	43	44	45			■	46						
47	48					■	49				■	■	■	■
50					■	51				■	52	53	54	55
56			■	57	58					59				
60			■	61					■	62				
63			■	64					■	65				

32. Triangular sail
34. Ill humor
35. Hive dwellers
37. Fashionable, '60s style
38. Union jack?
39. Alternatives
41. Magruder of Watergate
42. Chart
44. Japanese sash
45. Brimstone
46. Pamphlets
47. Hell
48. Part of the soft palate
49. Aladdin's friend
51. Not right
52. Arrive
53. Bucket
54. Dog of literature
55. Underworld river
58. Genetic material: abbr.
59. Pitch

Answers on page 88.

The But-Not Game

LANGUAGE VERBAL REASONING

The object of the "But-Not" Game is to uncover the element common to each statement.

Debbie likes seashells but not conchs.

Debbie likes bookshelves but not libraries.

Debbie likes cashews but not walnuts.

So … what does Debbie like?

Word Ladder

LANGUAGE PLANNING

Change just one letter on each line to go from the top word to the bottom word. Do not change the order of the letters. You must have a common English word at each step.

READ

______

______

______

BOOK

Answers on page 88.

Can't See the Trees for the Forest?

ATTENTION VISUAL SEARCH

Each set of words below contains the name of a tree. Can you find it? For example, the word "cloak" contains "oak," which is a type of tree.

1. Spine-tingling
2. Eyewitness
3. Clarence Darrow
4. Gospel music
5. Burma shave
6. Tea kettle
7. Shah of Iran
8. Naval architect

It's a Song

LANGUAGE

Can you "read" the phrase below?

N

O

O

M

D

A

B

Answers on page 88.

Training Exercise

PLANNING | SPATIAL REASONING

Run your train through the maze entering and exiting with the arrows. Remember: You can't back up, and you can't jump track at the crossovers—you must go straight through them.

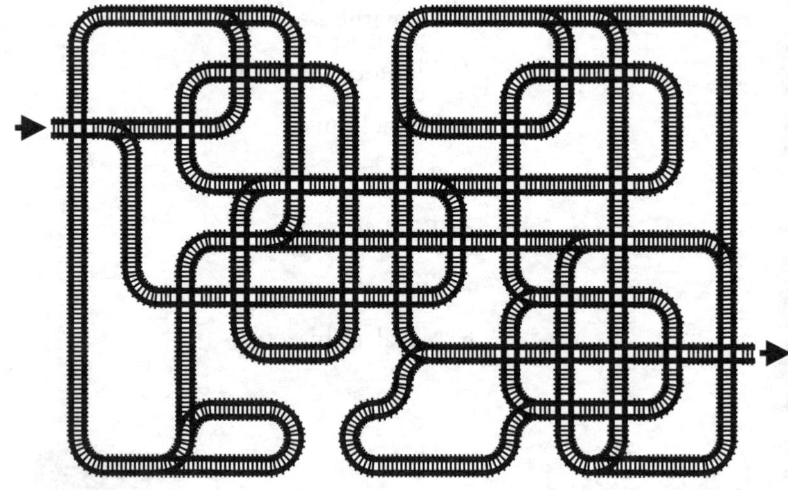

Answer on page 88.

Degrees of Confusion

LOGIC

In order to graduate with a prestigious degree from Existential University, philosophy majors have to answer one simple question on the final exam: What is at the end of time?

What is the correct answer to this one simple question that will give the philosophy majors their coveted degrees from old E.U.?

Rhyme Time: Why Fly

GENERAL KNOWLEDGE LANGUAGE

Answer each clue below with a pair of rhyming words. The numbers that follow each clue indicate how many letters are in each word. We've done the first one for you.

1. ". . . when you can go by train?" (3, 3): **why fly**
2. Question about wedding timing (3, 4): ____________
3. Prepare anklets for shipping (3, 5): ____________
4. Where most of the water goes out (4, 5): ____________
5. Interrupt sleep increasingly (5, 4): ____________
6. Heavyweight southpaw (5, 5): ____________
7. Where big ticket items are shown (5, 5): ____________
8. Eric the Red's men (5, 5): ____________
9. Barbecue that isn't used (5, 5): ____________
10. Uncles (7, 8): ____________

Answers on page 89.

Stretch Your Brain

Up and Over

PLANNING SPATIAL REASONING

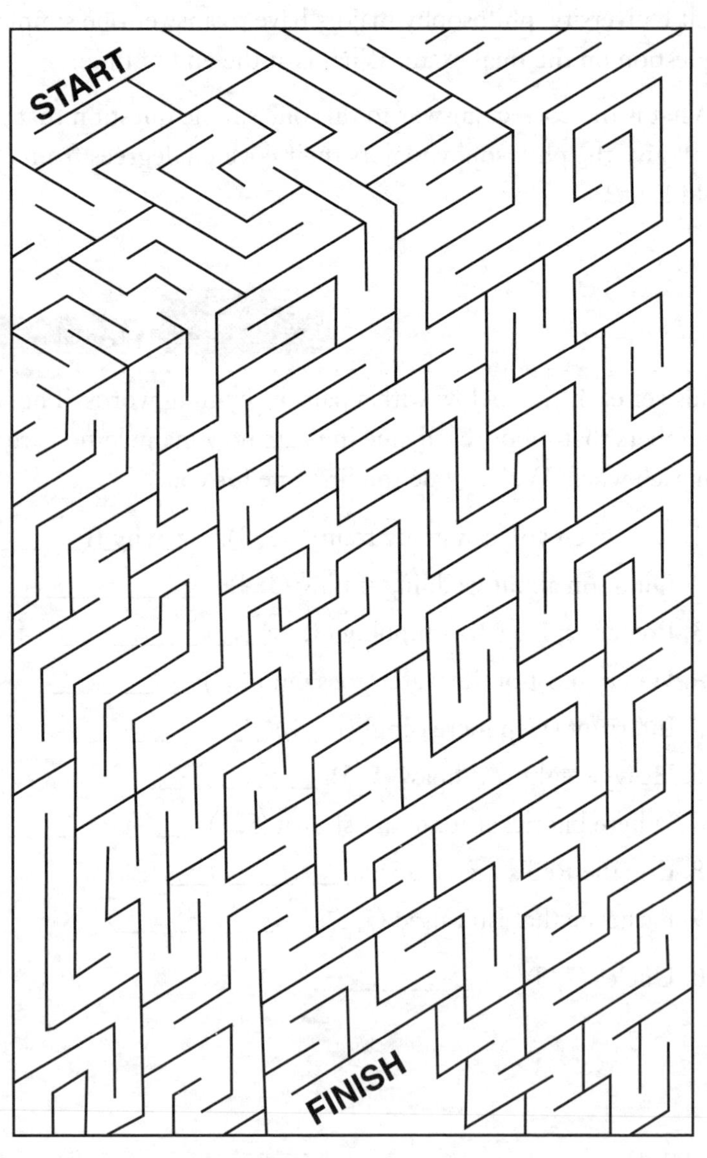

Answer on page 89.

Lottery Logic

COMPUTATION LOGIC

Gary, Hurley, and Joe pool their money every week to play the lottery. Gary puts in $3, Hurley puts in $2, Joe puts in $1. With this money, they buy 6 tickets. Because they put in different amounts and because Joe doesn't appear to be too bright, they decide to divide any winnings the following way: Gary would get one-half, Hurley would get one-third, and Joe would get one-ninth. The friends finally get a winner, and the prize is $34. The prize was paid in dollar bills, and none of them had any coins to make change. Gary and Hurley couldn't figure out how to divide the dollar bills in the pot. Joe reached into his pocket, pulled something out, and the friends were able to divide their winnings according to the agreed-upon deal. What did Joe pull out of his pocket?

Go Forth ... and Multiply!

COMPUTATION LOGIC

Fill each square of the grid with a digit from 1 through 9. When the numbers in each row are multiplied, you should arrive at the total in the right-hand column. When the numbers in each column are multiplied, you should arrive at the total on the bottom line. The numbers in each diagonal must multiply to the totals in the upper and lower right corners.

Important: The number 1 can only be used once in any row or column; other numbers can be repeated.

			24
	1		**12**
2		5	**40**
	3		**6**
16	**12**	**15**	**16**

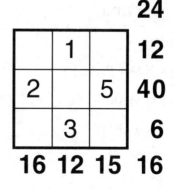

Answers on page 89.

MEET THE CHALLENGE

LEVEL 3

The State of Things

ATTENTION
LANGUAGE
VISUAL SEARCH

Every word or phrase listed is contained within the group of letters on the next page. The words can be found in a straight line horizontally, vertically, or diagonally. The words can be read either backward or forward.

Leftover letters spell the theme of this puzzle.

A HEN WHIMPERS
A HUT
BANKS ARE
COOL ROAD
GYM I OWN
HA! I DO!
I'M ACHING
I MEAN
IN NAVY PLANES
IT IS WAVERING
LAND ARMY
LEWD AREA
LOOK! A HAM!
NOMINATES
NOT A MAN
OLD FAIR
SO LAUNCH A RIOT
TAXES
TEEN SENSE
WE MIX ONCE
WINS COINS
WORN KEY

Level 3

L E V E R S Y Y O W H O N S E
O A F T E H E M I L N A O E S
E I N X T K C N A O D L I S A
N I A D N E S O M H A F I D S
A T N R A C E I O U A T A R O
N A O N O R N N N L I K E I G
E W G I A A M C S S R P O E R
R R N N T V H Y W E M O C O A
N S A E I A Y A N I N N A E L
A W S S R H V P H A O S R D M
T O O I K E C W L X M A E N F
T U O I R N N A I A D A A H E
N T H I M E A M M W N E T A M
E O N A H Y E B E I M E F O A
U G S A S W G L T I A T S E N

Answers on page 89.

Meet the Challenge

Two Rules

LANGUAGE LOGIC

Cryptograms are messages in substitution code. Break the code to read the message. For example, THE SMART CAT might be FVO QWGDF JGF if **F** is substituted for **T, V** for **H, O** for **E,** and so on.

Hint: Look for repeated letters. **E, T, A, O, N, R,** and **I** are the most-often-used letters. A single letter is usually **A** or **I;** OF, IS, and IT are common 2-letter words; THE and AND are common 3-letter groups.

HNMFM TFM HIG FPQMK WGF

PQHCJTHM KPAAMKK CO QCWM.

OMSMF HMQQ MSMFLHNCOY

LGP EOGI.

Answer on page 89.

Cube It!

COMPUTATION LOGIC

Fill in this crossword with numbers instead of letters. Use the clues to determine which numbers 1 through 9 belong in each square. No zeros are used.

ACROSS

1. A perfect cube that is a palindrome (reads the same backward as it does forward)
4. A multiple of 9
5. Its digits add up to 16
7. Its middle digit is the sum of its two outside digits

1	2	3	■
4			■
■	5		6
■	7		

DOWN

1. A multiple of 17
2. A palindrome
3. A number of the form ABAB
6. Its first digit is twice its last digit

Like a Candy Bar

LANGUAGE

Can you "read" the phrase below?

CNHUOTCSK

Answers on page 89.

Meet the Challenge

It's a Wrap!

Which one of the cubes is a correct wrap of the center pattern?

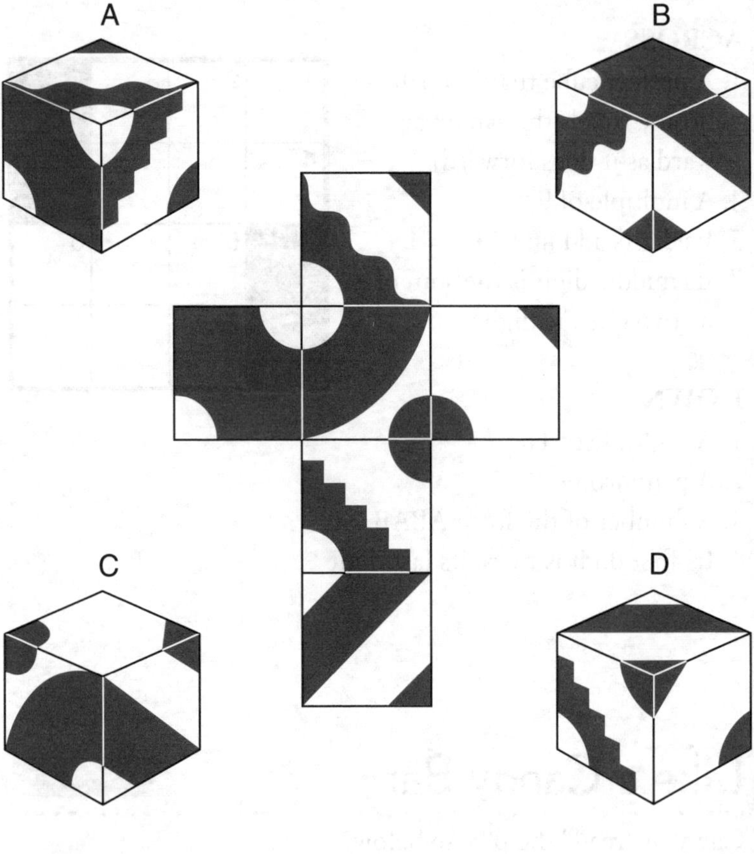

A

B

C

D

Answer on page 89.

What a Whistle (Part I)

MEMORY

Read the story that follows. Then turn the page for a quiz on what you've read.

When I was 14, I used to hang out at a nature center in Connecticut, where I grew up.

One day a man brought in a sparrow hawk with a busted wing. These days the official name of the bird is the American kestrel, but they will always be sparrow hawks to me. Anyway, it was a little beauty, a small falcon about the size of a jay, with beautiful colors—blue-gray wings, rufous tail and back—and that piercing gaze of hawks.

One of the curators, Les, took care of the sparrow hawk for a few months, feeding it small strips of raw meat. As the bird's wing grew stronger, Les started retraining it to fly indoors, holding a piece of meat in a gloved hand. He'd stand close at first, so the bird could practically jump to his hand, but then he'd stand farther and farther away. Soon the little hawk was flying to him for the food.

Each time Les held out the food, he'd do this remarkable whistle, which he said was the sound of a screech owl. It had a slightly eerie, tremulous sound. You do the whistle by fluttering the back of your tongue loosely against your palate. It's hard to explain. I practiced a lot, and soon I could do it too. People always seem surprised at the sound—it's not a typical whistle. You can vary the pitch to high or low by how you flutter your tongue. I don't have a lot of talents, but, by gum, I can do the screech-owl whistle!

Meet the Challenge

What a Whistle (Part II)

MEMORY

(Do not read this until you have read the previous page!)

1. In which state did the author grow up?
2. Another name for the "sparrow hawk" is:
   a) blue grouse
   b) American kestrel
   c) purple finch
3. How old is the author at the time of the story?
4. True or false: The sparrow hawk has greenish wings.
5. Sparrow hawks in captivity can be fed:
   a) celery
   b) potatoes
   c) raw meat
6. The sparrow hawk in the story had:
   a) a bad wing
   b) a broken leg
   c) missing tail feathers
7. The sparrow hawk, or kestrel, is a type of:
   a) shore bird
   b) falcon
   c) jay
8. As the bird healed, the curator:
   a) let it go
   b) retrained it to fly
   c) took it home
9. The curator trained the bird by using:
   a) a certain whistle
   b) a clucking sound
   c) a duck decoy
10. The sound the curator made was that of:
    a) a bald eagle
    b) a screech owl
    c) a barn owl

Answers on page 90.

A-Dissection

PLANNING | SPATIAL REASONING

Using just your eyes, can you divide the shape below into 3 equal parts? You can only "cut" along the lines of the grid. Shapes may be mirrored.

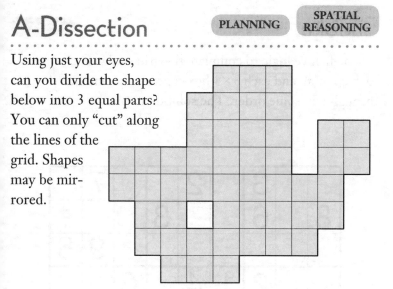

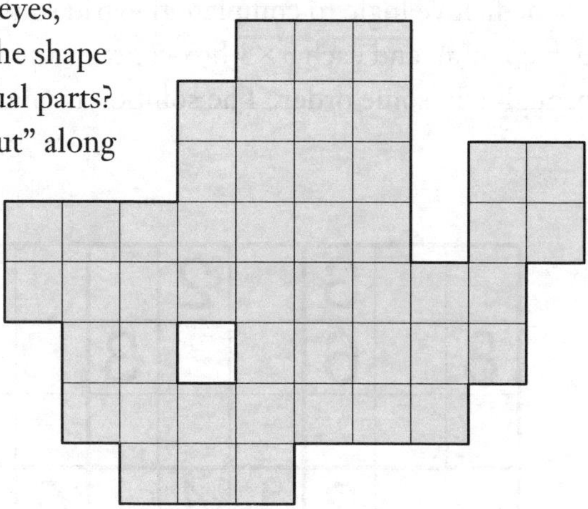

Push for the Pinnacle

COMPUTATION | LOGIC

Help the mountaineer reach the summit by filling the boulder circles with numbers. Each boulder is the sum (the total when added) of the 2 numbers in the boulders that support it. For example: 2+3=5. If a total is 10 or more, just write in the second digit. For example: 7+6=13; write in 3.

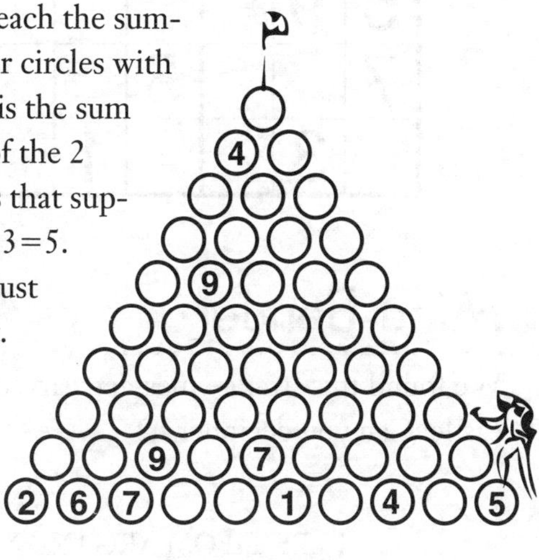

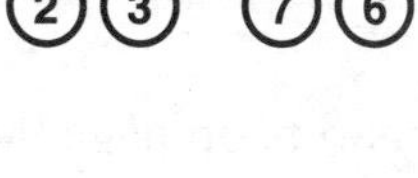

Answers on page 90.

Sudoku

LOGIC

Use deductive logic to complete the grid so that each row, each column, and each 3×3 box contains the numbers 1 through 9 in some order. The solution is unique.

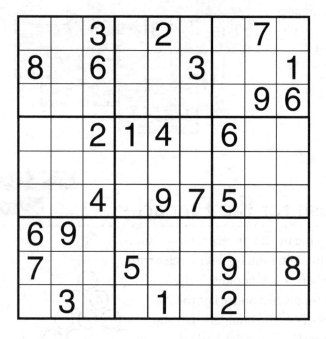

		3		2			7	
8		6			3			1
							9	6
		2	1	4		6		
		4		9	7	5		
6	9							
7			5			9		8
	3			1		2		

Mind-Bender

LANGUAGE LOGIC

We found this strange message carved on a rock in an ancient castle. Can you decipher it?

FLES TIFOM ARGAN ANASI ELF ITS

Answers on page 90.

Star Power

LOGIC

Fill each of the squares in the grid so that every green star is surrounded by a digit from 1 through 8 with no repeats.

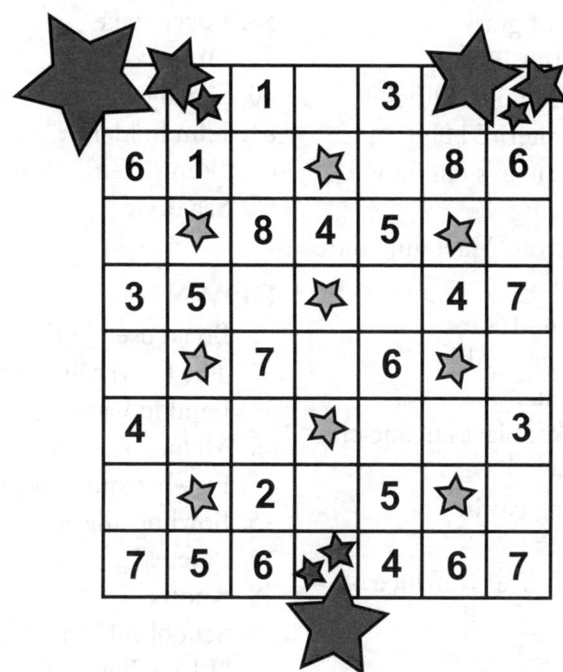

Travel Trouble

LOGIC

Bob and Rob are Siamese twins who always wanted to go on a vacation. Bob wanted to spend a week in Europe while Rob wanted to spend a week seeing the sights in China and Japan. Both left on the same day, returned seven days later, and managed to fulfill their individual travel wishes. How did they do it?

Answers on page 90.

Meet the Challenge

About Face

GENERAL KNOWLEDGE LANGUAGE

ACROSS

1. Intended course
5. Leaf of grass
10. Practice boxing
14. No friend to Othello
15. Hammerin' Hank
16. Superman's childhood pal Lang
17. Bancroft–MacLaine film: 3 wds.
20. Put in order
21. Be in accord
22. Cravats
23. Market places in ancient Rome
25. Riding clothes
28. Exacts
31. South Seas romance of 1847
32. Greased
33. Narrow inlet
35. Novel by John Marquand: 4 wds.
39. Spring collectors: abbr.
40. Eroded
41. "Planet of the _____"
42. Calmed with medication
44. Ancient Palestinian fortress
46. Organization: abbr.
47. Sing with great force
48. Look fixedly
51. Snakes
55. Lets the heat in: 4 wds.
58. Poker stake
59. Of space
60. Speedy animal
61. Film holder
62. "Funny Girl" Brice
63. Sea eagle

DOWN

1. Bread used in the East
2. The Cowardly Lion actor
3. Land in Caesar's day
4. Memo
5. Flat-bottomed boats
6. Bowling alleys
7. Parched
8. Knotts
9. School subject: abbr.
10. "I Like Ike," e.g.
11. Two of a kind
12. Bancroft or Boleyn
13. Evaluate
18. Part of a military group
19. Thanksgiving Day event
23. Wrong-doer
24. Hebrew measure
25. Mesa dwellers
26. Cupids in paintings
27. Capital of Idaho
28. Broke bread

29. Mountain dweller of Tibet
30. Begot
32. Frequently
34. Handle: Lat.
36. Raises the nap
37. Fare for Dobbin
38. "_____ luxury of woe" (Thomas Moore)
43. Type of grass
44. Just
45. Paradise for skiers
47. Irish playwright
48. Play the lead
49. Choreographer Tommy
50. Comedian Johnson
51. British carbine
52. At hand
53. Mountain lake
54. Pintail duck
56. Blockhead
57. Gun owners group: abbr.

Answers on page 90.

Meet the Challenge

Fold-O-Rama

PLANNING SPATIAL REASONING

Answer on page 91.

Rhyme Time: Wind Kind

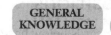

GENERAL KNOWLEDGE LANGUAGE

Answer each clue below with a pair of rhyming words. The numbers that follow each clue indicate how many letters are in each word. We've done the first one for you.

1. Old-fashioned watch (4, 4): **wind kind**
2. A dive over the line for a touchdown (4, 4): ___________
3. South Florida college residence (4, 4): ___________
4. Swindle on the tracks (4, 4): ___________
5. Specialized utensil (4, 4): ___________
6. Antique store purchase (4, 5): ___________
7. A most impressive bird of prey (5, 5): ___________
8. Peanut butter cookies (5, 5): ___________
9. Clique within the cast (6, 5): ___________
10. In-crowd's favorite flick (6, 5): ___________
11. Temporary crown (6, 6): ___________
12. Picnic pest counter (7, 5): ___________

Game Time

LANGUAGE

Can you "read" the phrase below?

INNING
INNING
INNING
INNING
INNING
INNING
I N N I N G

Answers on page 91.

Card Positions

LOGIC

The 4 playing cards below have been chosen from each of the 4 suits in a deck of cards. There is an ace, a king, a queen, and a jack. Assuming that the cards are facing you, determine the rank and suit of each card.

1. The ace is farther to the right than the spade.
2. The diamond is farther to the left than the queen, and the club is farther to the right than the queen.
3. The heart is farther to the left than the jack, and the spade is farther to the right than the jack.

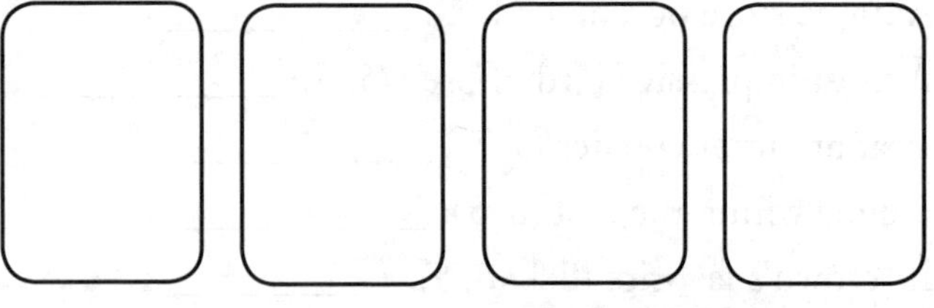

Initially Yours

GENERAL KNOWLEDGE LANGUAGE

We hope you don't come up short trying to figure out what these famous abbreviations stand for!

1. AKA, in a police report
2. BART, in San Francisco
3. FAQ, on a Web site
4. IBM
5. M*A*S*H
6. MSG, in food preparation
7. POTUS, in American government
8. PVC, the plastic used in some household pipes
9. SST, as in the Concorde SST
10. VCR

Answers on page 91.

Level 3

PLANNING

SPATIAL REASONING

Fourth Assembling

Each of the 16 square tiles shown in the illustration contains some part of the number 4. Select the 4 tiles that can create a 2×2 square so that a full "4" character appears on it. Tiles should not be rotated, flipped, or overlapped.

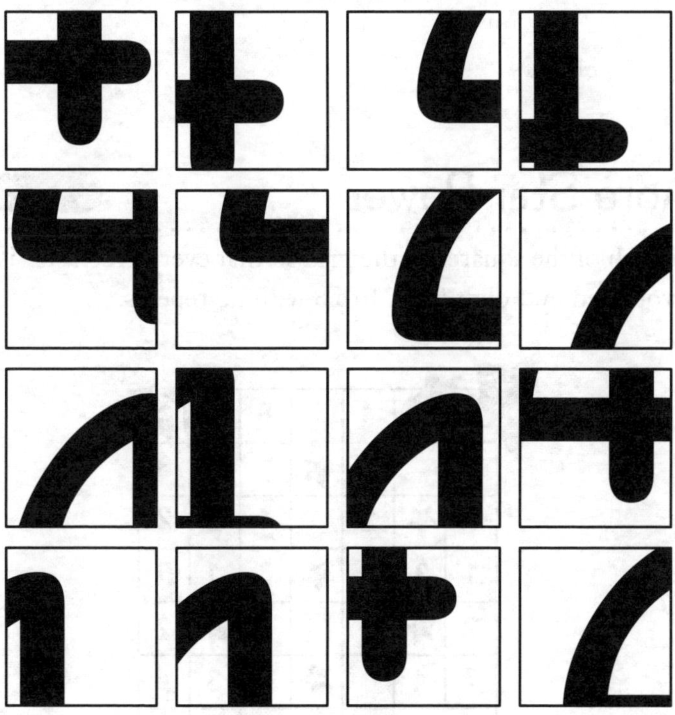

Answer on page 91.

Word Ladder

LANGUAGE PLANNING

Change just one letter on each line to go from the top word to the bottom word. Do not change the order of the letters. You must have a common English word at each step.

DRUM
______ African Palm tree
______ building where a number of people sleep
______ small, soft-bodied animal
______ used
HORN

More Star Power

LOGIC

Fill each of the squares in the grid so that every green star is surrounded by a digit from 1 to 8 with no repeats.

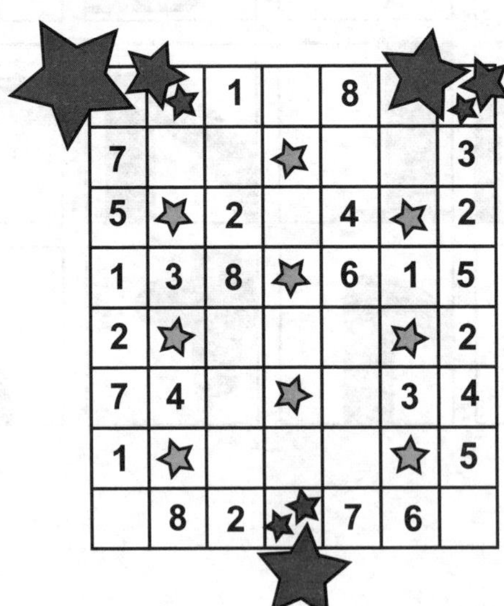

Answers on page 91.

Chess Squares

COMPUTATION LOGIC

How many squares are there all together on this standard chessboard?

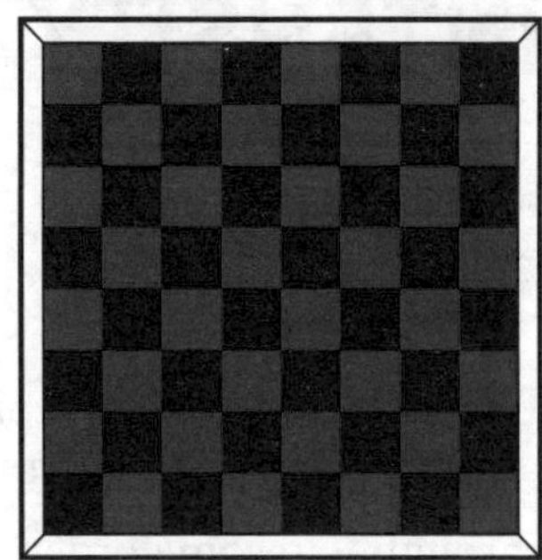

Rhyme Time: Slow Flow

LANGUAGE LOGIC

Answer each clue below with a pair of rhyming words. The numbers that follow each clue indicate how many letters are in each word. We've done the first one for you.

1. Plumbing problem (4, 4): **slow flow**
2. Entrée option (4, 4): ____________
3. Go on a road trip (4, 4): ____________
4. Obsessive one's objective (4, 4): ____________
5. Bovine that just ate (4, 4): ____________
6. "Jack and Jill" (4, 4): ____________
7. Trumpeter's oldest instrument (4, 4): ____________
8. Base stealer's maneuver (4, 5): ____________
9. Spectral party giver (5, 4): ____________
10. The "and" after "Four score" (5, 4): ____________
11. Equine army (5, 5): ____________
12. Pronouncement by U.S. Customs (6, 5): ____________
13. More irate snake (6, 5): ____________
14. Writer's advance (6, 6): ____________
15. Stronger snub (6, 8): ____________

Answers on pages 91–92.

Sudoku

LOGIC

Use deductive logic to complete the grid so that each row, each column, and each 3×3 box contains the numbers 1 through 9 in some order. The solution is unique.

	9					8	4	
3			7					5
		3		9			2	
	2		6		1		9	
	8			4		3		
1					5			6
	4	6					7	
		8						

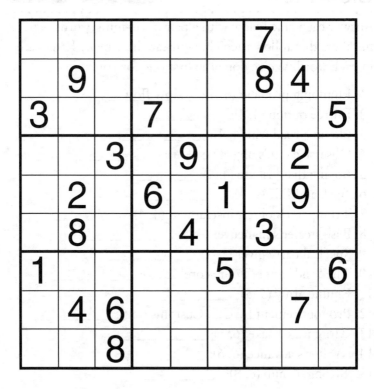

Answers on page 92.

Second Assembling

PLANNING SPATIAL REASONING

Each of the 9 squares shown in the illustration contains some part of the number 2. Select the 4 squares that can create a 2×2 square so that a full "2" character appears on it. Tiles should not be rotated, flipped over, or overlapped.

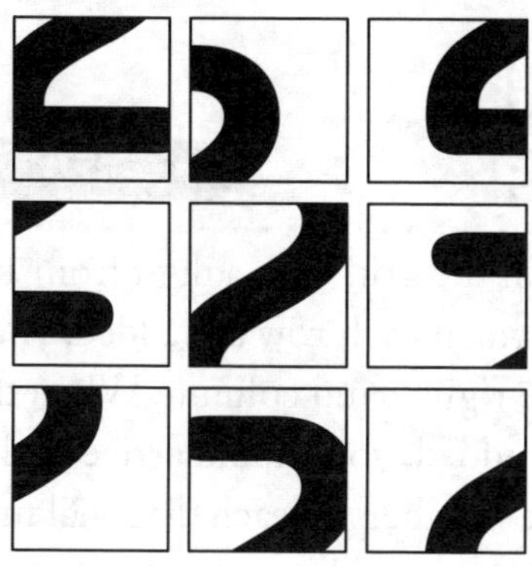

Word Ladder

LANGUAGE LOGIC

Change just one letter on each line to go from the top word to the bottom word. Do not change the order of the letters. You must have a common English word at each step.

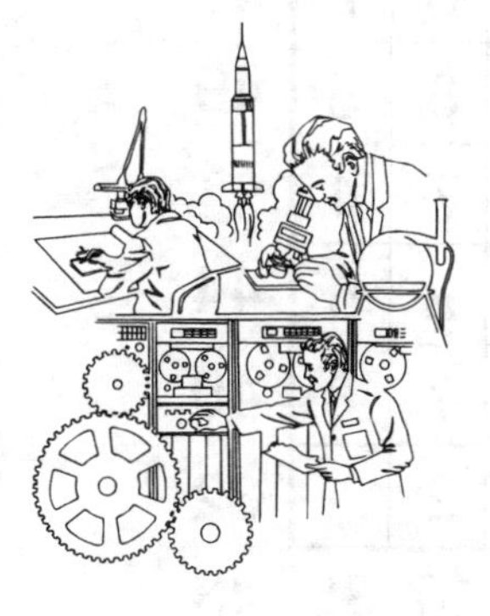

WORK

____

____

____

____

____

PLAY

Answers on page 92.

Hidden Names

ATTENTION · VISUAL SEARCH

Nine first names are hidden in the sentence below. What are they?

Alabama rye bread is dandy, but

anglophiles are used to automat toast.

ADDicted to Puzzles!

COMPUTATION · LOGIC

Fill each square in the grid with a digit from 1 through 9. When the numbers in each row are added, you should arrive at the total in the right-hand column. When the numbers in each column are added, you should arrive at the total on the bottom line. The numbers in each diagonal must add up to the totals in the upper and lower right corners.

								23
	7	2	5	4	7		1	31
2	6		4	7		3	4	40
9		8	4		2	6	7	47
4		6		2	6	8	5	49
7	1		6		9	7	4	41
6		5		8	5	2	5	44
		2	3		5	7	8	40
1	6	7	8	4		2		32
40	46	38	43	39	46	37	35	43

Answers on page 92.

Arrow Web

LOGIC SPATIAL PLANNING

Blacken some of the arrows so that each arrow in the grid points to exactly one black arrow.

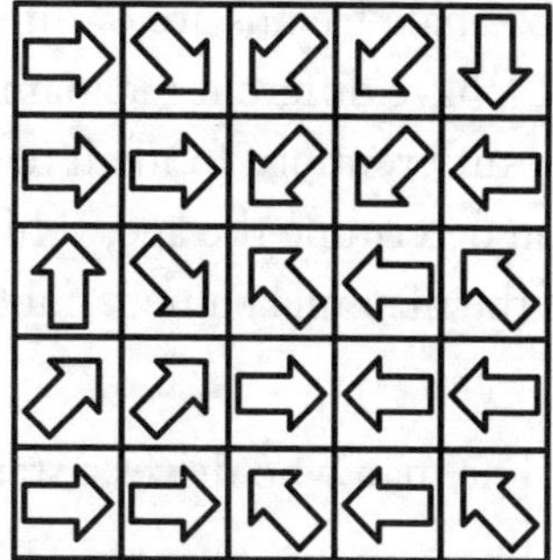

Rhyme Time: Why Try

GENERAL KNOWLEDGE LANGUAGE

Answer each clue below with a pair of rhyming words. The numbers that follow each clue indicate how many letters are in each word. We've done the first one for you.

1. Underachiever's credo (3, 3): **why try**
2. They make meals for the masses (4, 4): ____________
3. She can afford the best of brooms (4, 5): ____________
4. Attorney's excessive billing (4, 5): ____________
5. Aid for river crossers (4, 5): ____________
6. It's got a whistle too (5, 4): ____________
7. Time stopper (5, 4): ____________
8. They're hooked on omelets (6, 5): ____________
9. Revolutionary new pedal (6, 5): ____________
10. Require the study of poetry (6, 5): ____________
11. How to avoid dog bites (6, 6): ____________
12. Where to find roots (7, 5): ____________
13. Underachiever's credo (5, 8): ____________
14. In search of comic relief (5, 8): ____________
15. Monotonous tiles (6, 8): ____________

Answers on page 92.

Name that Nickname

LOGIC

Five male friends are of different ages, drive different vehicles, have different nicknames, have different jobs, and root for different pro football teams. Using the clues below, can you determine the age, vehicle, job, and favorite football team of the man nicknamed Tubba?

- The man who drives a station wagon roots for the Raiders.
- The man who drives a Hummer is 42.
- The man who roots for the Bengals is a flea trainer.
- The man who roots for the Cowboys has a 2-year age difference with the competitive eater.
- The man who drives an SUV is a toothpick tester.
- The man who drives an RV has a 2-year age difference with the 40-year-old.
- The man who roots for the Browns is nicknamed Dubba.
- The oldest man is 4 years older than the apple dewormer.
- The 38-year-old man roots for the Steelers.
- The man whose age is in the middle is an apple dewormer.
- The man nicknamed Rubba has a 2-year age difference with the man who roots for the Steelers.
- The man who drives an RV is the youngest.
- The 44-year-old man is a beer-bottle capper.
- The man who roots for the Cowboys has a 2-year age difference with the man nicknamed Hubba.
- The man who drives a pickup is nicknamed Bubba.

Answers on page 92.

Level 4

A Maze in Rose

PLANNING | SPATIAL REASONING

Connect the green dots in this Tudor rose.

Sound of Music

ANALYSIS | CREATIVE THINKING

Can you determine the missing letter in this logical progression?

D, R, M, F, ____, L, T, D

Answers on page 93.

T-Cubed Rectangles

SPATIAL REASONING

Four folding patterns are scattered around a 1×1×1 cube as shown in the illustration. Determine all those patterns that form a cube when folded along the lines. No parts of each cube should overlap each other.

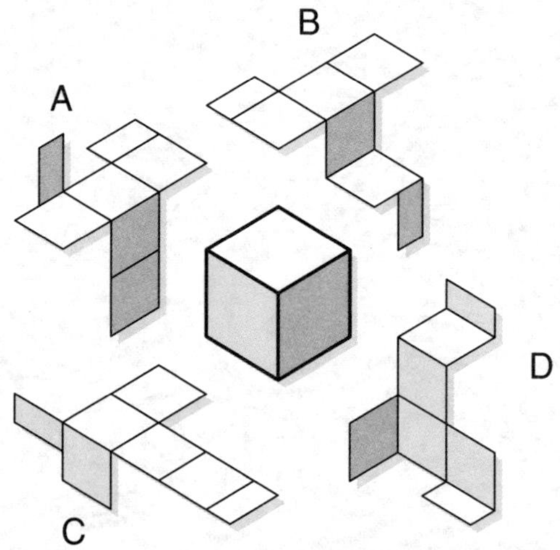

The Answer Man (Part I)

MEMORY

Read the following story. Then turn to page 64 and see whether you can correctly answer questions about what you've read.

Invictus Sigafoos was writing a book. Not just any book, mind you. This was *The Book of Answers.* It would be a guaranteed bestseller, he assured his friends, because it would have all the answers. "Got a question?" he said to his pal Eddie Shrdlu. "The answer is in the book."

"Come on, Vic," said Eddie. "Any question?"

"You got it, pal. Go ahead, ask a question."

Answers on page 93.

"Okay. What can go up a chimney down but not down a chimney up?"

"That's on page 3," said Vic. "An umbrella."

"All right," said Eddie. "Pretty good. Here's another one: What is the one 11-letter word that all Harvard graduates spell incorrectly?"

"Page 17," said Vic. " 'Incorrectly.' "

"I'm impressed!" said Eddie. "So if you know everything, tell me this: What is the meaning of life?"

"Everyone knows that," said Vic. "42."

"Page 42?"

"No, just 42. Didn't you read *The Hitchhiker's Guide to the Galaxy*?"

The book was published and became a bestseller, just as Invictus had predicted. On his book tour, he arrived in Milwaukee and went to the hotel he was supposed to be staying at—only to find there wasn't a room to be had. The place was sold out!

"But I have a reservation!" said Invictus.

"I'm sorry, sir," said the desk clerk. "Some people have extended their stays. We don't have a single room."

Invictus needed an answer, but this one wasn't in his book. He had to think fast. He was the Answer Man!

"So," he said to the desk clerk. "If the President of the United States was in town and needed a place to stay, are you telling me you wouldn't get him a room?"

"Well," said the desk clerk. "If it was the President, I'm sure we would find him a room somehow."

"Great!" said Invictus. "I'll take his room! He's not coming."

The Answer Man (Part II)

MEMORY

(Don't read this until you've read the previous page!)

1. What was the name of the president of the United States in 1980? (This is a trick question!)
2. What was the name of Eddie's book?
3. What city is named as being on the book tour?
4. What is the meaning of life?

Draw This!

SPATIAL VISUALIZATION

There's no trick here, only a challenge: Draw the mirror image of each of these familiar objects. You may find it harder than you think!

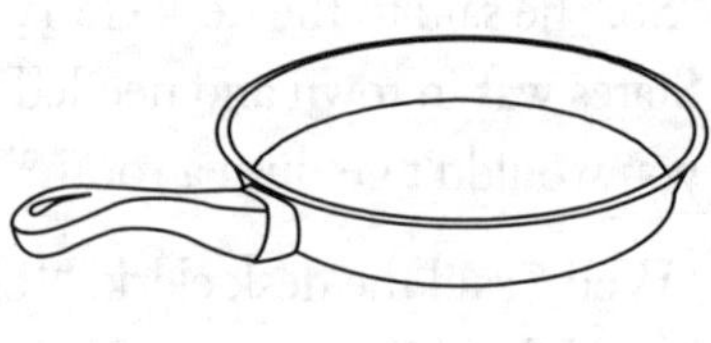

Answers on page 93.

Fill It In!

COMPUTATION LOGIC

Fill in this crossword with numbers instead of letters. Use the clues to determine which of the numbers 1 through 9 belongs in each square. No zeros are used.

Hint: Start with 5-Across, 6-Down, and 8-Across. Then look at 1-Down. The only 2-digit powers of two are 16, 32, and 64.

1	2		3	4
5		6		
	7			
8				9
10			11	

ACROSS

1. A prime number
3. A prime number
5. Consecutive digits, ascending
7. Its last digit is the sum of its first two digits
8. Consecutive digits, descending
10. Reversal of 3-Across
11. Eight more than 3-Across

DOWN

1. A power of 2 (i.e., a number in the doubling sequence 2, 4, 8, 16…)
2. In this five-digit number ABCDE, the two-digit number AB times C equals the two-digit number DE.
3. A palindrome
4. A composite (non-prime) number
6. Consecutive digits, ascending
8. A multiple of 3
9. A multiple of 7

Answers on page 93.

Increase the Intensity

GENERAL KNOWLEDGE

LANGUAGE

The International Scene

ACROSS

1. Ooze
5. Excuse
10. Soothing ointment
14. Summon
15. A difficulty or complication
16. Double-reed woodwind
17. They're fiercer than city apes: 2 wds.
20. Member speaking for the whole ball team: hyph.
21. Lacks
22. Enola
23. Untidy place
24. Performer
27. This gun for hire
33. Central part
34. Military barracks
35. Quilting party, perhaps

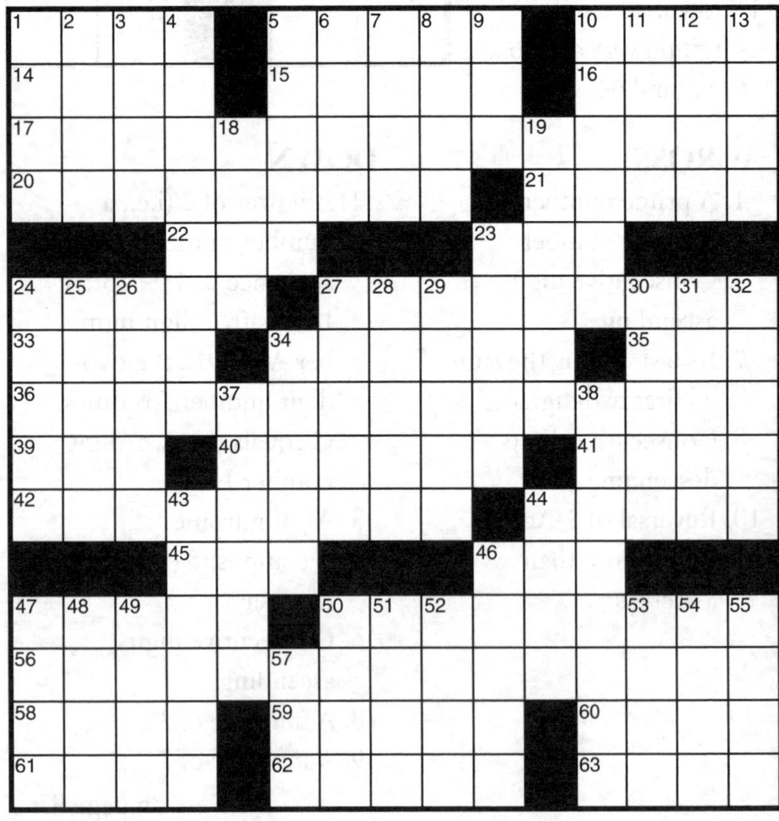

36. Countries just hatched: 2 wds.
39. Turn over the engine
40. National song
41. Quote or mention
42. White-collar bag
44. Cuts from copy
45. "_____ Were King"
46. Defeater of the Luftwaffe: abbr.
47. Nappy leather
50. Mermaids have them
56. Controlled by the military: 3 wds.
58. German river or dam
59. God's fishbowl
60. Peru's capital
61. Boys
62. Squeeze in
63. Observed

DOWN

1. Atlantic porgy
2. English noble
3. Noted island prison
4. Theater lover: hyph.
5. Quite incensed
6. Turn down: var.
7. Fixe or reçue: Fr.
8. Expel air
9. Middle East country: abbr.
10. Henry's Anne
11. Fit
12. Burden
13. Army meal
18. Close
19. Meaning
23. Beat it!
24. Sharp and biting
25. Person on way to success
26. Famous fountain of Rome
27. Devilfish
28. Baltic natives
29. Opera's Fleming
30. Seething
31. French income
32. Affirmatives
34. Beatrice, "The Beautiful Parricide"
37. Lighting director
38. Chunks dropping off glaciers
43. Downy ducks
44. Computer input or output
46. Class of German wines
47. Takes to court
48. Loosen a knot
49. Happy place
50. Confront
51. Steamed
52. Men only
53. Mr. Nastase
54. Feeble, as an excuse
55. Singer of one last song
57. Shorten the grass

Answers on page 93.

Increase the Intensity

Before and After

ATTENTION LANGUAGE VISUAL SEARCH

This 3-part puzzle is a fill-in-the-blank game, a word search, and a hidden message hunt. First, use the clues to find a word that completes the first word/phrase and begins the second. For example, the answer to Clue 1 would be "butterfly" because there's a Monarch butterfly and a butterfly kiss. The number of blanks tells you the number of letters in each missing middle word. (Hint: The missing words are in alphabetical order.) As you go along, circle the missing words, which are all hidden in the butterfly-shape word search grid. The words can be found in a straight line horizontally, vertically, or diagonally. If you can't figure out a missing word from the clues, look for words in the grid, which will help you solve the fill-in-the-blank portion of the puzzle.

Once you've circled all the words in the grid, read the uncircled letters in order from top to bottom to uncover a hidden message. The hidden message is an appropriate observation about certain commercials you see on TV.

CLUES

1. Monarch	_ _ _ _ _ _ _ _ _	kiss
2. Happy as a	_ _ _ _	chowder
3. Lincoln	_ _ _ _ _ _ _ _ _ _ _	drift
4. Tennis	_ _ _ _ _	jester
5. Way off in the	_ _ _ _ _ _ _ _	runner
6. Long	_ _ _ _ _ _ _ _	of labor
7. Body	_ _ _ _ _ _	jeopardy
8. Roman	_ _ _ _ _ _ _	penguin
9. The king's	_ _ _ _ _ _ _	muffin
10. Go	_ _ _ _ _ _	of speech

11. Fencing	_ _ _ _ _ _	of ceremonies
12. U.S.	_ _ _ _	sesame
13. Golden	_ _ _ _ _ _ _ _ _ _ _	knocks
14. Surprise	_ _ _ _ _	pooper
15. Picture	_ _ _ _ _ _ _	pitch
16. Strip	_ _ _ _ _	face
17. That's a good	_ _ _ _ _ _ _ _	mark
18. Downward	_ _ _ _ _ _	notebook
19. Acorn	_ _ _ _ _ _	racquet
20. Bumper	_ _ _ _ _ _ _	shock
21. Nylon	_ _ _ _ _ _ _ _	stuffer
22. I.Q.	_ _ _ _	tube
23. Doubting	_ _ _ _ _ _	Aquinas
24. Denzel	_ _ _ _ _ _ _ _ _ _	Post

			S							I			
				T					N				
N	N				I			E				A	E
L	O	L				C	P				T	M	N
H	I	O	Y	N		O	K		Y	S	P	E	G
T	S	E	T	B	O	N	E	E	T	E	C	F	L
O	I	R	I	B	U	T	T	E	R	F	L	Y	I
E	V	Q	N	A	N	I	G	O	A	D	A	A	S
F	I	G	U	R	E	N	R	N	P	D	M	F	H
	D	T	T	E	T	E	S	P	I	R	A	L	
			R	H	S	N	L	S	E	H			
	R	C	O	U	R	T	T	B	Q	A	S	D	
S	M	M	P	N	O	A	I	C	U	U	B	A	O
D	A	Y	P	O	N	L	E	O	E	O	A	V	W
S	S	T	O	C	K	I	N	G	N	F	D	S	E
R	T	L	E	O		E	O		K	S	R	W	H
O	E	R				S	R				E	E	A
F	R					T	E					R	P

Answers on page 93.

TRAIN YOUR BRAIN

Logic: Movie Weekend

LOGIC

Skip and Sissy are avid movie fans. But they live so far from a town with movie theaters that when they're in town for a weekend, they try to see as many films as possible. Last weekend they saw movies on Saturday night and Sunday night, as well as matinees on both days. They went to all 4 theaters in town: the Bijou, the Jewel, the Odeon, and the Plaza. The 4 movies were directed by Woody Allen, Robert Altman, Mel Brooks, and François Truffaut. The movies were as different as their directors: a comedy, a mystery, a science fiction, and a western. Using the information given below, determine when and where Skip and Sissy saw each film and who directed it.

1. Skip and Sissy saw the science-fiction movie later than the comedy but earlier than the movie playing at the Jewel. None of these films was directed by Robert Altman.
2. They didn't go to a matinee at the Plaza.
3. They saw the Woody Allen film later than the comedy and earlier than the Truffaut movie, but none of these 3 films played at the Bijou.
4. They saw the Mel Brooks movie later than the western.

	BIJOU	JEWEL	ODEON	PLAZA	COMEDY	MYSTERY	SCIENCE FICTION	WESTERN	ALLEN	ALTMAN	BROOKS	TRUFFAUT
SAT. MATINEE												
SAT. NIGHT												
SUN. MATINEE												
SUN. NIGHT												
ALLEN												
ALTMAN												
BROOKS												
TRUFFAUT												
COMEDY												
MYSTERY												
SCIENCE FICTION												
WESTERN												

Answers on page 94.

Digitile

SPATIAL REASONING

Shade the tiles of this grid so that the numbers 0 through 9 are represented. Each shaded figure must contain its representing digit in the grid. Figures can be rotated but not reflected. Figures will be 5 squares tall and 3 squares wide and cannot overlap. We've done the first one for you.

Note: It is not necessary to shade ALL the grid squares.

			0				5				
	8										
							7				
											6
			1								
					4						
2						3				9	

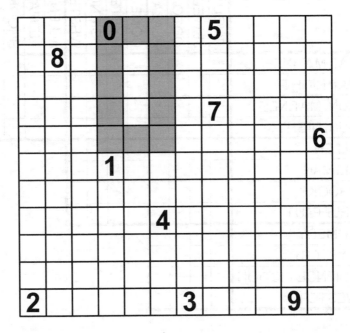

Season's Greetings

ANALYSIS CREATIVE THINKING

Can you determine the missing letter in this logical progression?

D, D, P, V, C, ___, D, B

Answers on page 94.

It's a Shore Thing (Part 1)

ATTENTION MEMORY VISUAL SEARCH

This private beach has an unusual entrance "fee": Before you can use the beach, you've got to take a memory test given by the beach patrol. Study this picture for 2 minutes, then turn the page and answer the 10 questions. Seven or more right answers gets a free beach permit for the day!

It's a Shore Thing (Part II)

MEMORY ATTENTION VISUAL SEARCH

(Do not read this until you have read the previous page!)

The beach patrol asks you the following questions:

1. What toy were the kids in the water throwing?

   ____

2. What was the girl with the braids holding?

   ____

3. What was the name of the lotion the woman was putting on her leg?______________________

4. What was the design on the swimsuit that same woman was wearing? ______________________

5. What kind of animal was the float in the water shaped like? ______________________

6. What was the name of the sailboat? ______________________

7. What had the angler caught? ______________________

8. What 3 types of clothing were worn by the man holding hands with his wife? ______________________

9. What does the lifeguard have slung over his arm?

   ____

10. How many birds were in the picture? ______________________

Answers on page 94.

Level 5

Rhyme Time: Bran Fan

GENERAL KNOWLEDGE

Answer each clue below with a pair of rhyming words. The numbers that follow each clue indicate how many letters are in each word. We've done the first one for you.

1. She favors one cereal type (4, 3): **bran fan**
2. Inquiry about a Middle East itinerary (3, 5): __________
3. Following homework assignment (4, 4): __________
4. Lights on the runway (5, 5): __________
5. Motionless vibrato (5, 5): __________
6. Following an appliance cycle (5, 5): __________
7. Source of a little light (5, 5): __________
8. Small band performing Cuban dance music (5, 5): __________
9. Their team just won the Super Bowl (5, 5): __________
10. Part of a "Star Trek" episode (5, 5): __________
11. What the ray was moved in (5, 5): __________
12. Move the herd (6, 5): __________
13. "It's time to stop shopping!" (6, 5): __________
14. Add air after balloon's early landing (7, 4): __________
15. Supposedly cushy job that wasn't (4, 8): __________
16. Music scholarship contestant's finale (5, 7): __________
17. Temporary tool source (6, 6): __________
18. He's chilled out (6, 6): __________
19. Supervisor in the Inferno (8, 5): __________
20. Tool for illegal immigration control (6, 8): __________

Answers on page 94.

In Other Words (Anagrams)

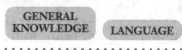

GENERAL KNOWLEDGE | LANGUAGE

ACROSS

1. Literary collection
4. Ruin's partner
9. Rebuke
13. Decrease
15. Consumed
16. A little, in music
17. Greedy
18. Got up
19. Type of chamber
20. Notarial cheater, in other words: 2 wds.
23. Overjoy
24. Final
25. Free
28. Listens to
33. Sweep's foe
37. Ruler on the Rialto
40. Actor Davis
41. Mutilate scepter, in other words: 2 wds.

44. Marie Antoinette, e.g.
45. Jannings or Ludwig
46. Tibetan oxen
47. Plus
48. Pinch
50. Koufax stats: abbr.
54. Odor
59. Braille primrose, in other words: 2 wds.
65. Country on the Caspian
66. Like some skirts
67. Dross
68. Average: hyph.
69. Growing out
70. Bingo kin
71. Mound builders
72. Stymie
73. NYSE purchase: abbr.

DOWN

1. Cognizant
2. Of the seagoing service
3. Loos or O'Day
4. End of dependence
5. _____ avis: Lat.
6. Semicircular island
7. Jai alai equipment
8. On hands and _____
9. Risky investment: abbr.
10. Arm of a firth
11. Feel every muscle
12. Down and out
14. Emend
21. Poet's "above"
22. One of 3 swordsmen
26. Mt. _____, Crete
27. Love lavishly
29. Spot
30. On the main
31. Casablanca nightclub owner
32. Complete outfits
33. Koran section
34. Cheers for Ferdinand
35. "Miss _____ Regrets"
36. Prong
38. Precious stone
39. Land of loughs
42. Foot, for Frost
43. Actor Wallach
49. Anderson or Tillis
51. Stormed
52. Favorite Garbo word
53. Jack of rhyme
55. Take a chance
56. Famous Canadian physician
57. Signified
58. Peloponnesian city
59. Mona _____
60. _____ horse
61. Phloem
62. Grandson of the first family
63. Network
64. Baltic feeder

Answers on page 94.

Multiples of Six Number Maze

COMPUTATION | SPATIAL VISUALIZATION

Find your way through the maze. Start with the hexagon containing a 6 on the left, and finish with the hexagon containing a 6 on the right. Move from hexagon to hexagon only if there is a line connecting them, and only pass through hexagons containing multiples of 6.

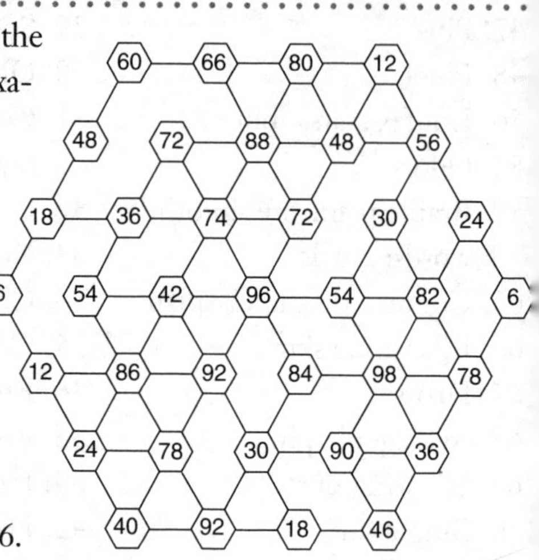

Chip off the Old Block

PERCEPTION | SPATIAL VISUALIZATION

Is **A, B, C, D,** or **E** the missing piece from the broken cube? Try to solve this with your eyes only.

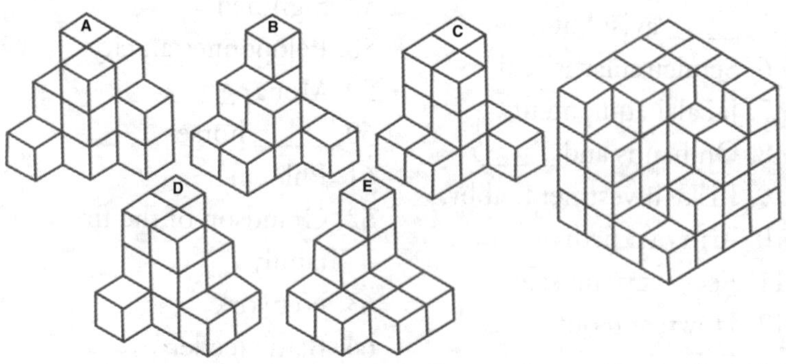

Answers on page 94.

Animal Names

LANGUAGE PROBLEM SOLVING

Cryptograms are messages in substitution code. Break the code to read the message. THE SMART CAT might become FVO QWGDF JGF if **F** is substituted for **T**, **V** for **H**, **O** for **E**, and so on. Look for repeated letters. **E, T, A, O, N, R,** and **I** are the most-often-used letters. The code is the same for each of these animal names.

1. TMDDQDQKCLNX
2. TCLXKVY
3. UMQJ
4. FMYCHHV
5. YCIIMK
6. LQNJKCMJ FQCK
7. VUVDTCJK
8. QDQXXNL
9. LQQXY
10. YTMJQOVYQX

A Honey of a Puzzle

MEMORY RECALL

Answer each definition with a six-letter word. Write the words clockwise around the numerals in the grid. Words overlap each other and may start in any of the spaces around the numerals. To assist you, we've placed some of the letters.

1. ___ the Pooh
2. Flowers from Holland
3. Struck lightly
4. Successful contestant
5. Escaped notice
6. More rosy
7. Two ___ don't make a right
8. Ukrainian port
9. Hot spring

Answers on page 95.

Word Ladder

LANGUAGE LOGIC

Change just one letter on each line to go from the top word to the bottom word. Do not change the order of the letters. You must have a common English word at each step.

TINY

____

____

____

____

____

HUGE

Sudoku

LOGIC

Use deductive logic to complete the grid so that each row, each column, and each 3×3 box contains the numbers 1 through 9 in some order. The solution is unique.

			5				3	1
4				8		7		
9		6		1				
					3		6	
		4				9		
	5		4					
				4		1		8
		8		3				7
2	7				5			

Answers on page 95.

Rhyme Time: Hot Lot

GENERAL KNOWLEDGE LANGUAGE

Answer each clue below with a pair of rhyming words. The numbers that follow each clue indicate how many letters are in each word. We've done the first one for you.

1. Prime and priced to sell (3, 3): **hot lot**
2. Surfers (3, 3): ________________
3. Perceive a rustle in the woods (4, 4): ________________
4. Wrestler's innovative tactic (4, 4): ________________
5. There's an "a" and a "b" on a 1040 (4, 4): ________________
6. Feature of Saturn (4, 5): ________________
7. Public square in the Middle East (4, 5): ________________
8. Goes overboard in the meat section (5, 5): ________________
9. Get a 10 in the winter Olympics (5, 5): ________________
10. Demonstrate frustration, in a way (5, 6): ________________
11. Worrisome warble (6, 5): ________________
12. Travel guide's article (6, 6): ________________
13. Accidental sighting (6, 6): ________________
14. Why the mummy wasn't there (7, 7): ________________
15. It came from the wooden sled (6, 8): ________________

Answers on page 95.

SUMsational!

COMPUTATION LOGIC

Fill each square in the grid with a digit from 1 through 9. When the numbers in each row are added, you should arrive at the total in the right-hand column. When the numbers in each column are added, you should arrive at the total on the bottom line. The numbers in each diagonal must add up to the totals in the upper and lower right corners.

								35
1		4	3	1		6	5	29
2	3	1	4			5	8	35
4	2	6		2	7	8		43
2	3		7	6	1		4	31
1	6			5	7	8	5	42
3	5	3	8		4		2	39
		8	7	5	3		3	34
	8	7	5	9		4	1	41
18	34	38	48	38	41	43	34	29

Answers on page 95.

Level 5

ATTENTION

LANGUAGE

VISUAL SEARCH

Number Please

This word find differs from the norm. You will not search for the actual digits in the word list. Instead, you'll search for the spelling of each digit within each word. The first word, for example, is BALFOUR. All of the words have numbers within them, though they may not sound like that number when pronounced.

```
N O I S N E T T O G R O F I V
S E I T N E V E S N T D L O T
S I S O T H P R G H E I G E N
A T D I O L I V G L I R N F E
T N H L X D E I C O R D O O X
U F E G D S E E Y D E O R U Y
R R O G I L H E C R F O U R S
N E M O S E N O L R O W O R I
I I O K B O H O O E W T F A X
N G N E M N I T N T T F L G P
E H E E V N G B E E E I A E E
L T T L P O R T N C B R B R N
I E A O F I V E F O L D C E C
G R R E N I N H C Y R T S O E
D E Y I N S E S N E V E L E L
```

BAL 4 (Earl of)
CYCL 1
DRIF 2 OD
11SES
5 FOLD
FORGOT 10
FR 8 ER
H 8 S
L 1 SOME
M 1 TARY
M 1 Y
9 PINS
N 1
1 ROUS
ROT 10
SATUR 9
7 TIES
6 PENCE
6-SHOOTER
SL 8
STRYCH 9
10 DERLOIN
10 SION
2 FER
UND 1

Answers on page 95.

Third Assembling

PLANNING SPATIAL REASONING

Each of the 12 tiles shown in the illustration contains some part of the number 3. Select the 4 tiles that can create a 2×2 square so that a full "3" character appears on it. Tiles should not be rotated, flipped, or overlapped.

A Bright Idea

LOGIC

A billionaire offered 3 men this challenge: "The man who can fill this room with something using the least amount of money will win a million dollars." The first man spent $100 and filled the room with lots of air-filled balloons. The second man spent $10 dollars and filled the room with a single, giant air-filled balloon. The third man spent nothing and won the million dollars. What did he do?

Answers on page 95.

ANSWERS

Crosswise (page 6)

```
          E C O R C
          S Y O S U
          S S S C H
          O O A R L
          R L S O S
N R O T C C R O S S W I N D S
C R E E R I F S S O R C U C I
F Y U D M A A E W R R N K I N
D L U P C C O Y I C N C A C R
B O S S O R C E S E T L A M S
          O O S E L
          S S S O B
          T F O S U
          I G R O O
          C L C D D
```

It Figures (page 7)

			19
2	1	7	**10**
3	4	9	**16**
8	5	6	**19**
13	**10**	**22**	**12**

Dry Your Eyes (page 7)

Don't cry over spilled milk.

In a Stew (page 8)

carrot, turnip, pasta, potato, seasoning, leek, chicken, celery

Thinking Outside the Bubbles (page 8)

Thanksgiving

Number Climber (page 9)

It's Thrilling! (page 9)

sudden death overtime

Colorful Phrases (page 10)

1. red carpet
2. orange blossom
3. yellow pages
4. green thumb
5. blue chip
6. purple finch
7. brown rice
8. black belt

Word Ladder (page 10)

Answers may vary.

HATE, date, dote, dove, LOVE

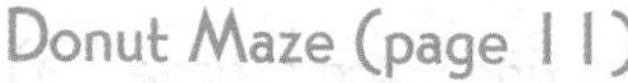

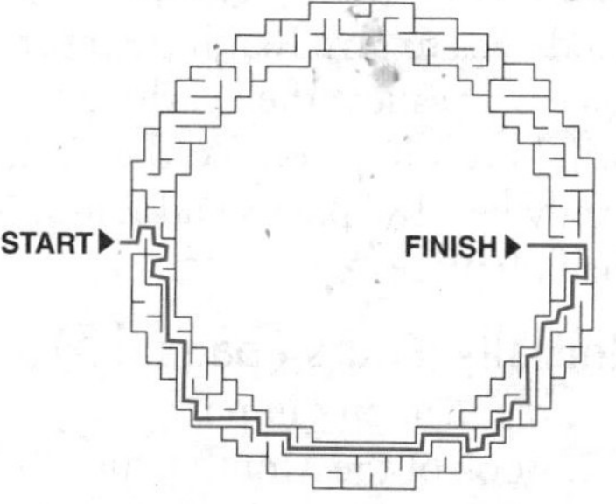

Zoo Story (pages 12–13)

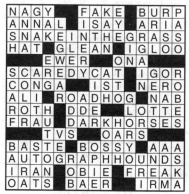

N	A	G	Y			F	A	K	E		B	U	R	P
A	N	N	A	L		I	S	A	Y		A	R	I	A
S	N	A	K	E	I	N	T	H	E	G	R	A	S	S
H	A	T		G	L	E	A	N		I	G	L	O	O
			E	W	E	R			O	N	A			
S	C	A	R	E	D	Y	C	A	T		I	G	O	R
C	O	N	G	A			I	S	T		N	E	R	O
A	L	I		R	O	A	D	H	O	G		N	A	B
R	O	T	H		D	D	E			L	O	T	T	E
F	R	A	U		D	A	R	K	H	O	R	S	E	S
			T	V	S			O	A	R	S			
B	A	S	T	E		B	O	S	S	Y		A	A	A
A	U	T	O	G	R	A	P	H	H	O	U	N	D	S
I	R	A	N		O	B	I	E		F	R	E	A	K
O	A	T	S		B	A	E	R			I	R	M	A

Rhyme Time: See Me (page 14)

1. see me; 2. top cop; 3. fat bat; 4. chow now; 5. last cast or past cast; 6. pony crony; 7. mars tsars; 8. wrong thong; 9. coffee toffee; 10. sports reports

Times Square (page 14)

5	2	5	1	50
1	2	3	3	18
5	2	1	2	20
5	1	3	7	105
125	8	45	42	

Counting Candy (page 15)

Andy has to give Randy 40 more pieces of candy; then each boy will have 120 pieces. At the start, Andy had 180 pieces and Randy had 60 pieces.

Initially Yours (page 15)

1. big man on campus
2. Book of the Month Club
3. cash on delivery
4. extra-sensory perception
5. high-definition television
6. machine-groomed snow
7. patrol torpedo
8. standing room only
9. unidentified flying object
10. water displacement

Really Sum-thing (page 16)

			9
7	9	3	19
8	1	4	13
5	2	6	13
20	12	13	14

Go for the Gourd (page 16)

GOmer GOt the urge to draG Out an orange GOurd even though it wasn't Halloween. He carved his own face (which shows that his eGO was a biG One!). GOmer GOt more GOurds and carved a GOose with GOut, an egG On a wall, and a ganG Of GOrillas GOing ape. He showed them to his gal Gloria, a former GO-GO dancer who was now a biG Old GOurd grower from Georgia. She gave GOmer a baG Of seeds to grow more GOurds and GO whole-hoG Out on his porch carving them.

21 Is a "Sharp" Number (page 17)

Time Will Tell (page 17)

wait and see

A-MAZE-ing Race (page 18)

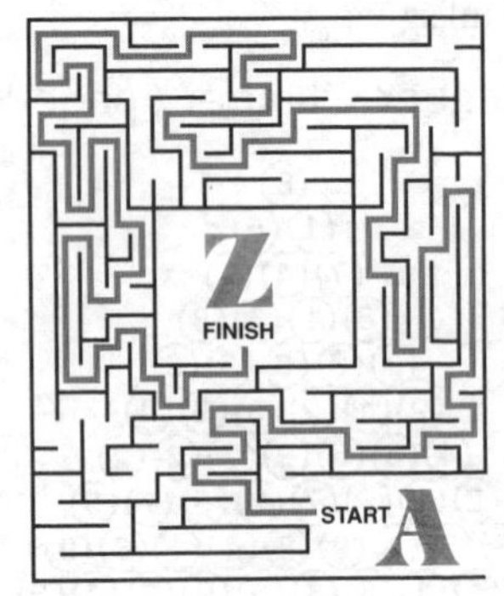

True or False (page 19)

1. 4+5=8 is false.
2. 3+11=14 is true.
3. 22−19=2 is false.
4. 15+16=31 is true.
5. 90−12=88 is false.
6. 45−40=46 is false.
7. 7+11=18 is true.
8. 80−20=70 is false.
9. 70+13=83 is true.
10. 31−21=12 is false.

Initially Yours (page 20)

1. Baltimore & Ohio
2. Cooperative for American Relief Everywhere
3. electrocardiogram (or -graph)
4. Greenwich Mean Time
5. International Standard Book Number
6. light-emitting diode
7. National Aeronautics and Space Administration
8. répondez, s'il vous plaît
9. surface-to-air missile
10. sealed with a kiss

Word Ladder (page 20)

Answers may vary.
DOVE, love, lore, lure, lurk, LARK

Spinning in Circles (page 21)

Crisscross Puzzle (pages 22-23)

Zen in a Nutshell (page 24)

Be here now. Be someplace else later. Is that so complicated?

The But-Not Game (page 24)

Carol likes words with "her" in them.

Reach the "Sum"mit (page 25)

Food for Thought (pages 26–27)

Theme: Each word or expression includes a word that is a type of cake.

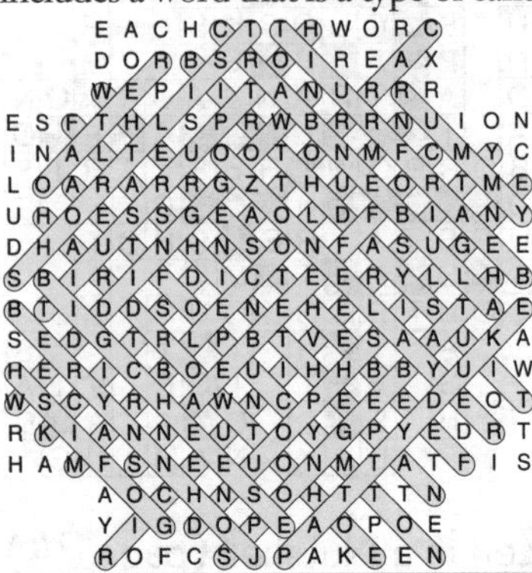

Making Music (page 28)

download songs

The Times Tables Are Turned! (page 29)

			75
2	3	5	30
4	5	4	80
3	1	2	6
24	15	40	20

Picnic Puzzle (page 29)

No! It's impossible to cover the remaining tablecloth squares with the hoagies. Draw an 8×8 checkerboard with alternating red-and-white squares. When you draw a pitcher of lemonade covering the diagonal corners, you will be covering either two red or two white squares (let's say red). When you put a hoagie on the table, it must cover a red and a white square. But there are now 32 white squares and only 30 red ones. Sally won't be able to do it.

Breakfast's Ready (pages 30–31)

The But-Not Game (page 32)

Debbie likes words with "she" in the middle of them.

Word Ladder (page 32)

Answers may vary.

READ, road, rood, rook, BOOK

Can't See the Trees for the Forest? (page 33)

1. pine; 2. yew; 3. cedar; 4. elm; 5. ash; 6. teak; 7. fir; 8. larch

It's a Song (page 33)

bad moon rising

Training Exercise (page 34)

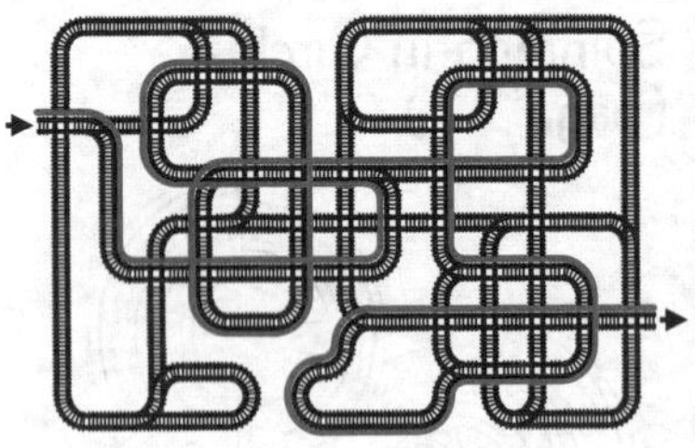

Degrees of Confusion (page 35)

The letter **E** is at the end of time.

Rhyme Time: Why Fly (page 35)

1. why fly; 2. why July; 3. box socks; 4. main drain; 5. snore more; 6. hefty lefty; 7. store floor; 8. Norse force; 9. still grill; 10. mother's brothers

Up and Over (page 36)

Lottery Logic (page 37)

Joe reached into his pocket and pulled out 2 more dollar bills. He added them to the pot, making the total \$36. Then the pot could be divided. Gary got one-half of \$36, or \$18. Hurley got one-third of \$36, or \$12. Joe got one-ninth of \$36, or \$4. \$18+\$12+\$4=\$34. Joe took the leftover \$2 and put it back in his pocket.

Go Forth ... and Multiply! (page 37)

			24
4	1	3	12
2	4	5	40
2	3	1	6
16	12	15	16

The State of Things (pages 38–39)

Leftover letters spell: "Everyone of these is an anagram of the named U.S. state."

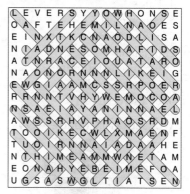

L	E	V	E	R	S	Y	Y	O	W	H	O	N	S	E
O	A	F	T	E	H	E	M	I	L	N	A	O	E	S
E	I	N	X	T	K	C	N	A	O	D	L	I	S	A
N	I	A	D	N	E	S	O	M	H	A	F	I	D	S
A	T	N	R	A	C	E	I	O	U	A	T	A	R	O
N	A	O	N	O	R	N	N	N	L	I	K	E	I	G
E	W	G	I	A	A	M	C	S	S	R	P	O	E	R
R	R	N	N	T	V	H	Y	W	E	M	O	C	O	A
N	S	A	E	I	A	Y	A	N	I	N	N	A	E	L
A	W	S	S	R	H	V	P	H	A	O	S	R	D	M
T	O	O	I	K	E	C	W	L	X	M	A	E	N	F
T	U	O	I	R	N	N	A	I	A	D	A	A	H	E
N	T	H	I	M	E	A	M	M	W	N	E	T	A	M
E	O	N	A	H	Y	E	B	E	I	M	E	F	O	A
U	G	S	A	S	W	G	L	T	I	A	T	S	E	N

Two Rules (page 40)

There are two rules for ultimate success in life. Never tell everything you know.

Cube It! (page 41)

3	4	3	■
4	7	7	■
■	7	3	6
■	4	7	3

Like a Candy Bar (page 41)

chock-full of nuts

It's a Wrap! (page 42)

The answer is **B.**

What a Whistle (pages 43–44)

1. Connecticut
2. b) American kestrel
3. 14
4. False
5. c) raw meat
6. a) a bad wing
7. b) falcon
8. b) retrained it to fly
9. a) a certain whistle
10. b) a screech owl

A-Dissection (page 45)

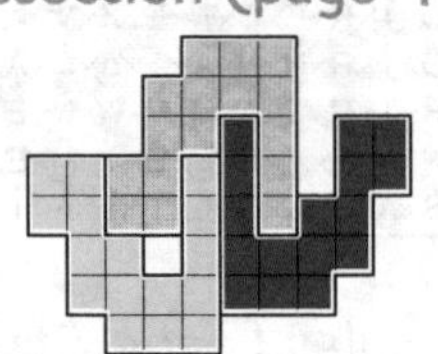

Push for the Pinnacle (page 45)

Sudoku (page 46)

9	1	3	4	2	6	8	7	5
8	5	6	9	7	3	4	2	1
2	4	7	8	5	1	3	9	6
5	7	2	1	4	8	6	3	9
3	8	9	2	6	5	7	1	4
1	6	4	3	9	7	5	8	2
6	9	5	7	8	2	1	4	3
7	2	1	5	3	4	9	6	8
4	3	8	6	1	9	2	5	7

Mind-Bender (page 46)

Read the message backward—and put spaces in the right places—and you'll see that it says "Stifle is an anagram of itself," a bit of self-referential humor that really is a mind-bender!

Star Power (page 47)

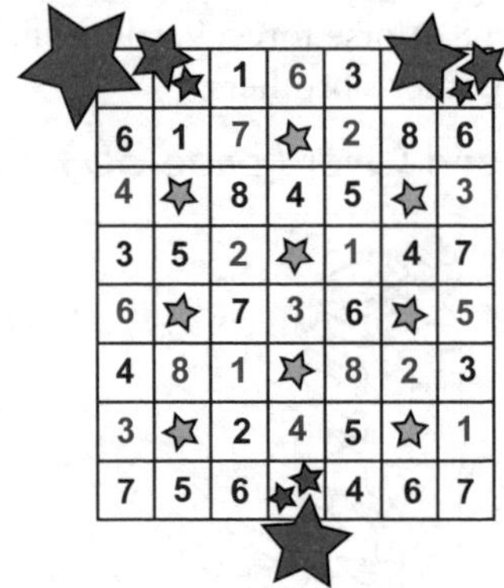

Travel Trouble (page 47)

Bob and Rob are Siamese twins, but they are not attached to each other.

About Face (pages 48–49)

P	L	A	N	■	B	L	A	D	E	■	S	P	A	R
I	A	G	O	■	A	A	R	O	N	■	L	A	N	A
T	H	E	T	U	R	N	I	N	G	P	O	I	N	T
A	R	R	A	N	G	E	D	■	■	A	G	R	E	E
■	■	■	T	I	E	S	■	F	O	R	A	■	■	■
H	A	B	I	T	S	■	D	E	M	A	N	D	S	■
O	M	O	O	■	■	O	I	L	E	D	■	R	I	A
P	O	I	N	T	O	F	N	O	R	E	T	U	R	N
I	R	S	■	E	A	T	E	N	■	■	A	P	E	S
■	S	E	D	A	T	E	D	■	M	A	S	A	D	A
■	■	■	A	S	S	N	■	B	E	L	T	■	■	■
S	T	A	R	E	■	■	S	E	R	P	E	N	T	S
T	U	R	N	S	O	N	T	H	E	S	T	E	A	M
A	N	T	E	■	A	R	E	A	L	■	H	A	R	E
R	E	E	L	■	F	A	N	N	Y	■	E	R	N	E

Fold-O-Rama (page 50)

Rhyme Time: Wind Kind (page 51)

1. wind kind; 2. hard yard; 3. warm dorm; 4. tram scam; 5. pork fork; 6. rare chair; 7. regal eagle; 8. sweet treat; 9. troupe group; 10. groovy movie; 11. dental rental; 12. skeeter meter

Game Time (page 51)

seventh-inning stretch

Card Positions (page 52)

king of hearts, jack of diamonds, queen of spades, ace of clubs

Initially Yours (page 52)

1. also known as
2. Bay Area Rapid Transit
3. frequently asked question
4. International Business Machines
5. Mobile Army Surgical Hospital
6. monosodium glutamate
7. President of the United States
8. polyvinyl chloride
9. supersonic transport
10. videocassette recorder

Fourth Assembling (page 53)

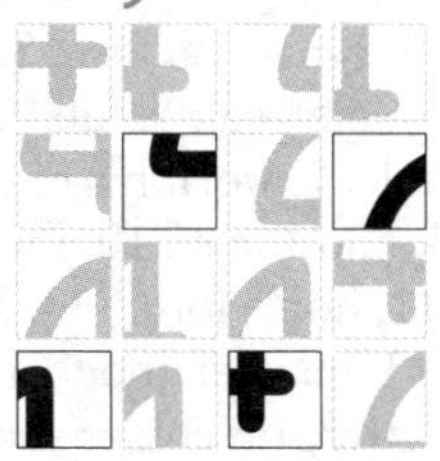

Word Ladder (page 54)

Answers may vary.
DRUM, doum, dorm, worm, worn, HORN

More Star Power (page 54)

☆	☆	1	5	8	☆	☆
7	4	6	☆	7	8	3
5	☆	2	3	4	☆	2
1	3	8	☆	6	1	5
2	☆	5	1	7	☆	2
7	4	6	☆	8	3	4
1	☆	3	4	2	☆	5
5	8	2	☆	7	6	1

Chess Squares (page 55)

There are 204 squares in all:
1×1 squares=64
2×2 squares = 49
3×3 squares=36
4×4 squares=25
5×5 squares=16
6×6 squares=9
7×7 squares=4
8×8 square=1

Rhyme Time: Slow Flow (page 55)

1. slow flow; 2. fish dish; 3. play away; 4. sole goal; 5. full bull; 6. pail tale; 7. worn horn; 8. wide slide; 9. ghost host; 10. third word; 11. horse force; 12. border order; 13. madder adder; 14. better letter; 15. colder shoulder

Sudoku (page 56)

8	5	1	3	2	4	7	6	9
2	9	7	1	5	6	8	4	3
3	6	4	7	8	9	2	1	5
4	1	3	5	9	8	6	2	7
7	2	5	6	3	1	4	9	8
6	8	9	2	4	7	3	5	1
1	3	2	4	7	5	9	8	6
9	4	6	8	1	3	5	7	2
5	7	8	9	6	2	1	3	4

Second Assembling (page 57)

Word Ladder (page 57)

Answers may vary.

WORK; pork; perk; peak; peat; plat; PLAY

Hidden Names (page 58)

al, mary, dan, andy, phil, les, ed, tom, matt

ADDicted to Puzzles! (page 58)

								23
3	7	2	5	4	7	2	1	**31**
2	6	5	4	7	9	3	4	**40**
9	5	8	4	6	2	6	7	**47**
4	9	6	9	2	6	8	5	**49**
7	1	3	6	4	9	7	4	**41**
6	9	5	4	8	5	2	5	**44**
8	3	2	3	4	5	7	8	**40**
1	6	7	8	4	3	2	1	**32**
40	**46**	**38**	**43**	**39**	**46**	**37**	**35**	**43**

Arrow Web (page 59)

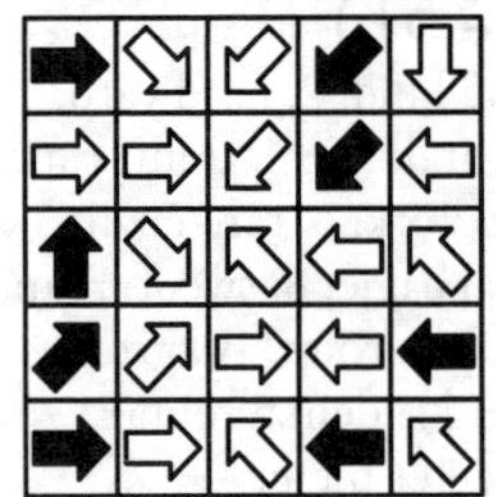

Rhyme Time: Why Try (page 59)

1. why try; 2. stew crew; 3. rich witch; 4. time crime; 5. ford board; 6. swell bell; 7. clock lock; 8. brunch bunch; 9. clever lever; 10. coerce verse; 11. muzzle puzzle; 12. beneath teeth; 13. never endeavor; 14. after laughter; 15. boring flooring

Name that Nickname (page 60)

The man nicknamed Tubba is 44. He drives a station wagon, is a beer-bottle capper, and roots for the Raiders.

A Maze in Rose (page 61)

The International Scene (pages 66–67)

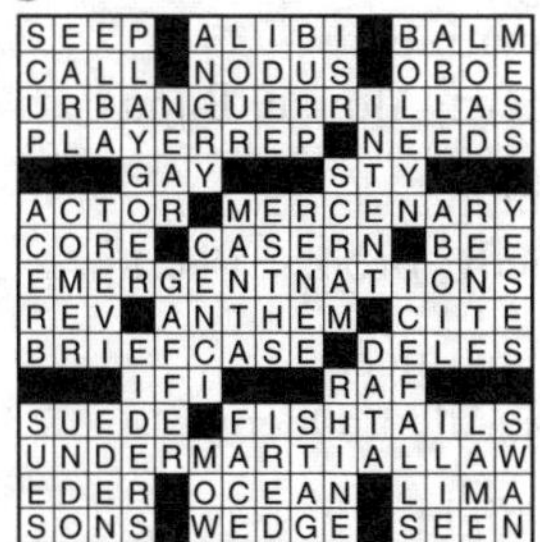

Sound of Music (page 61)

The missing letter is **S,** as in "so." The sequence: Do re mi fa so la ti do.

T-Cubed Rectangles (page 62)

B and **C** form cube when folded.

The Answer Man (pages 62–64)

1. The president of the United States had the same name in 1980 that he has today. (Told you it was a trick question!)
2. Eddie didn't write the book, Invictus did. (Egad, tricked again!)
3. Milwaukee.
4. 42, of course

Fill It In! (page 65)

3	7	■	3	1
2	3	4	5	6
■	1	5	6	■
8	7	6	5	4
1	3	■	3	9

Before and After (pages 68–69)

1. Butterfly
2. Clam
3. Continental
4. Court
5. Distance
6. Division
7. Double
8. Emperor
9. English
10. Figure
11. Master
12. Open
13. Opportunity
14. Party
15. Perfect
16. Poker
17. Question
18. Spiral
19. Squash
20. Sticker
21. Stocking
22. Test
23. Thomas
24. Washington

			S							I			
				T					N				
N	N				I			E				A	E
L	O	L				C	P				T	M	N
H	I	O	Y	N		O	K		Y	S	P	E	G
T	S	E	T	B	O	N	E	E	T	E	C	F	L
O	I	R	I	B	U	T	T	E	R	F	L	Y	I
E	V	Q	N	A	N	I	G	O	A	D	A	A	S
F	I	G	U	R	E	N	R	N	P	D	M	F	H
	D	T	T	E	T	E	S	P	I	R	A	L	
			R	H	S	N	L	S	E	H			
	R	C	O	U	R	T	T	B	Q	A	S	D	
S	M	M	P	N	O	A	I	C	U	U	B	A	O
D	A	Y	P	O	N	L	E	O	E	O	A	V	W
S	S	T	O	C	K	I	N	G	N	F	D	S	E
R	T	L	E	O		E	O		K	S	R	W	H
O	E	R				S	R				E	E	A
F	R					T	E					R	P

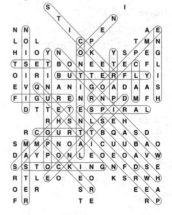

Leftover letters spell: In all those before-and-after ads, nobody ever looks worse after.

Logic: Movie Weekend (pages 70–71)

Sat. matinee:
Western; Altman; Bijou

Sat. night:
Comedy; Brooks; Plaza

Sun. matinee:
Sci-fi; Allen; Odeon

Sun. night:
Mystery; Truffaut; Jewel

Digitile (page 72)

Season's Greetings (page 72)

The missing letter is **C,** as in "Cupid." The sequence: Dasher, Dancer, Prancer, Vixen, Comet, Cupid, Donder, Blitzen

It's a Shore Thing (pages 73–74)

1. flying disc; 2. conch shell; 3. Goop; 4. stripes; 5. crocodile; 6. Breeze; 7. lobster; 8. shorts, jacket, hat; 9. megaphone; 10. four

Rhyme Time: Bran Fan (page 75)

1. bran fan; 2. why Dubai; 3. next text; 4. glide guide; 5. still trill; 6. since rinse; 7. porch torch; 8. mambo combo; 9. proud crowd; 10. space chase; 11. skate crate; 12. change range; 13. enough stuff; 14. inflate late; 15. poor sinecure; 16. vital recital; 17. renter center; 18. mellow fellow; 19. midlevel devil; 20. border recorder

In Other Words (Anagrams) (pages 76–77)

A	N	A			W	R	A	C	K		S	L	A	P
W	A	N	E		E	A	T	E	N		P	O	C	O
A	V	I	D		A	R	O	S	E		E	C	H	O
R	A	T	I	O	N	A	L	T	E	A	C	H	E	R
E	L	A	T	E			L	A	S	T				
				R	I	D				H	E	A	R	S
S	O	O	T		D	O	G	E		O	S	S	I	E
U	L	T	I	M	A	T	E	R	E	S	P	E	C	T
R	E	I	N	E		E	M	I	L		Y	A	K	S
A	S	S	E	T				N	I	P				
				E	R	A	S			A	R	O	M	A
L	I	B	E	R	A	L	P	R	O	M	I	S	E	R
I	R	A	N		G	O	R	E	D		S	L	A	G
S	O	S	O		E	N	A	T	E		K	E	N	O
A	N	T	S		D	E	T	E	R			R	T	S

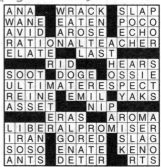

Multiples of Six Number Maze (page 78)

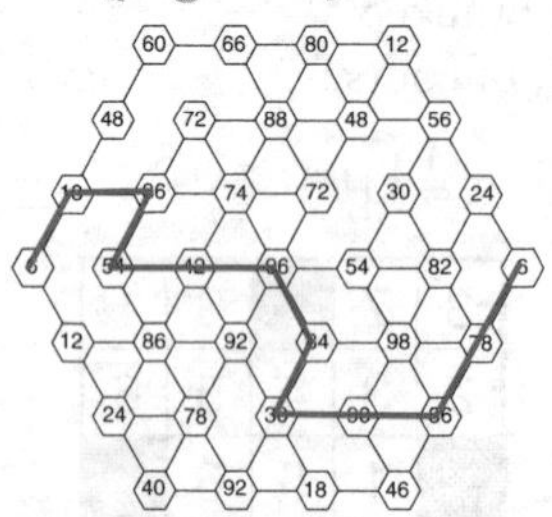

Chip off the Old Block (page 78)

The correct piece is **D.**

Animal Names (page 79)

1. hippopotamus; 2. hamster; 3. lion; 4. giraffe; 5. rabbit; 6. mountain goat; 7. elephant; 8. opossum; 9. moose; 10. rhinoseros.

A Honey of a Puzzle (page 79)

Word Ladder (page 80)

Answers may vary.
TINY, tins, tons, togs, tugs, hugs, HUGE

Sudoku (page 80)

7	8	2	5	9	6	4	3	1
4	1	5	3	8	2	7	9	6
9	3	6	7	1	4	2	8	5
8	9	7	1	2	3	5	6	4
1	2	4	6	5	8	9	7	3
6	5	3	4	7	9	8	1	2
3	6	9	2	4	7	1	5	8
5	4	8	9	3	1	6	2	7
2	7	1	8	6	5	3	4	9

Rhyme Time: Hot Lot (page 81)

1. hot lot; 2. wet set; 3. hear deer; 4. bold hold; 5. line nine; 6. ring thing; 7. Gaza plaza; 8. grabs slabs; 9. skate great; 10. pound ground; 11. shrill trill; 12. resort report; 13. chance glance; 14. history mystery; 15. winter splinter

SUMsational! (page 82)

								35
1	5	4	3	1	4	6	5	**29**
2	3	1	4	3	9	5	8	**35**
4	2	6	8	2	7	8	6	**43**
2	3	5	7	6	1	3	4	**31**
1	6	4	6	5	7	8	5	**42**
3	5	3	8	7	4	7	2	**39**
4	2	8	7	5	3	2	3	**34**
1	8	7	5	9	6	4	1	**41**
18	**34**	**38**	**48**	**38**	**41**	**43**	**34**	**29**

Number Please (page 83)

Third Assembling (page 84)

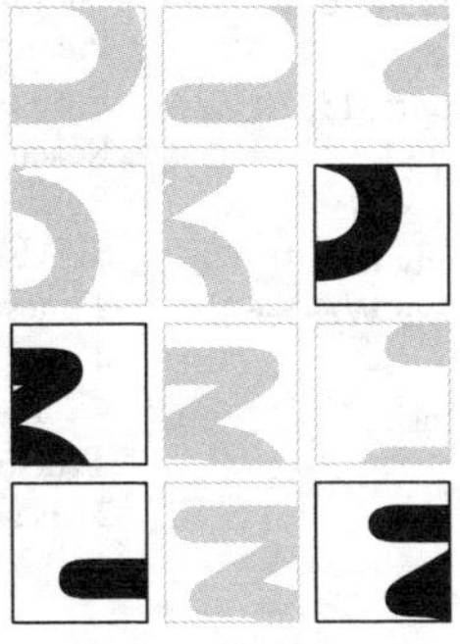

A Bright Idea (page 84)

He flipped a switch and filled the room with light.

INDEX